Dear Crossroads Supporter

Back in June, we offered the book, *"The Daniel Prayer: Prayer That Moves Heaven and Changes Nations"* by Anne Graham Lotz, to our partners who requested it at the time of their gift to our ministry.

Since then, we've experienced such significant financial turmoil that we were unable to ship your copy to you.

First, we sincerely ask your forgiveness for the delay in getting your book to you.

Next, we want you to know that God has now blessed us with the finances to be able to ship your book out to you, without delay.

Finally, we want to say, "Thank you...from the bottom of our hearts," for your faithful and continued support during this time, and for hanging in with us as we weathered this storm.

Now, we ask that you continue to keep the financial wellbeing of this ministry in your prayers, and encourage you to keep a lookout for your copy of "The Daniel Prayer," which should be arriving in your mailbox very soon.

With warmest regards,

Your Crossroads /100 Huntley Street Family

Anne is a natural, gifted teacher of *truth*. She also has a lifetime of experience from which she humbly yet boldly proclaims God's Word and wisdom. Now she does it once again in *The Daniel Prayer*. And once again she encourages us that we can move mountains too!

Kathie Lee Gifford

Readers who yearn for the restoration of America's cultural values will be tremendously inspired by Anne Graham Lotz's brilliant and moving insights. As one who has a deep desire to enhance the passion of her prayers, I find *The Daniel Prayer* to be an extremely powerful and motivational book that you cannot put down.

Senator Elizabeth Dole

When Anne Graham Lotz speaks, I listen. When she speaks on prayer, I lean in! In this great new book, a preeminent modern-day pray-er explores the prayer of one of the Bible's greatest intercessors. It is a marvelous combination that promises to challenge, inspire, and convict its readers. I enthusiastically recommend it.

Richard Blackaby, coauthor of *Experiencing God: Revised Edition*

As more Americans are turning away from the Lord, my friend Anne Graham Lotz has written a timely book about the power of prayer. In *The Daniel Prayer*, Anne argues we can renew, restore, and revive our nation—*if*—we agree to start praying like Daniel. I wholeheartedly agree! In *The Daniel Prayer* we come to understand we too can live and breathe the amazing power of prayer.

Gretchen Carlson, bestselling author and award-winning host of *The Real Story with Gretchen Carlson* on the Fox News Channel

I love this woman—her passion, courage, and listening ear. About fifty pages into *The Daniel Prayer*, Anne writes, "You and I will never know how to pray in such a way that Heaven is moved and our nation is changed until we start reading our Bibles." With that, Anne takes us into His Word and explains from Scripture, personal experience, and the lives of others the whole process of preparing for, pleading for, and prevailing in prayer. Then understanding our frailty when it comes to prayer (don't we all feel it!), Anne gives us practical help and direction for praying *The Daniel Prayer*. In Daniel 9:23, God told Daniel he was "highly esteemed—precious" and that is what my friend Anne is to me. And that is what we can be to God if we will but listen, obey, and pray.

Kay Arthur, cofounder of Precept
Ministries International and author of *Lord,
Teach Me to Pray in 28 Days*

Anne Graham Lotz has obviously spent a lot of time in prayer because in her latest book, *The Daniel Prayer*, she speaks with an authority that is not her own, that is bold and compelling and beautiful. This book may change your life because it will actually make you want to pray. Imagine that. It's true.

Eric Metaxas, *New York Times* bestselling
author and nationally syndicated radio host

America is in trouble because we have turned our back on God. Judgment is coming, and no earthly institution can save us. The only thing that will stay the hand of God from sending the destruction that we have brought on ourselves through our disobedience is prayer. With this book, Anne reminds us how a teenager-turned-prime-minister changed the fate of a nation through deeply intense and powerfully intentional prayer. *The Daniel Prayer* is an essential and timely read for a world on the eve of destruction. May we too, like Daniel, cry out, "O Lord, listen! O Lord, forgive! O Lord, hear and act!"

Janet Parshall, nationally syndicated
radio host

If you have a deep longing to see God move in our generation in an unprecedented way, then read *The Daniel Prayer*. It will break up the fallow ground in your heart, creating a yearning for God that only God Himself can fulfill. Thank you, Anne Graham Lotz, for this incredible book that has the capacity to lead us into a God-shaking moment in this world.

Dr. Ronnie Floyd, President, Southern
Baptist Convention and Senior Pastor,
Cross Church

Read this book and you will discover that prayer is not simply a part of Anne's life; it *is* her life. She explains why the prayer of Daniel should be our model for praying and, on that basis, allows us into her own heart, revealing her disappointments, her victories, and above all, her burden for our nation. As you read this book, let Anne's burden become yours!

Dr. Erwin W. Lutzer, Pastor Emeritus, the
Moody Church, Chicago

As a Jewish believer in Yeshua, the Messiah, as a son of the tribe of Judah and a direct descendant of the same Israelites who lived during the days of the prophet Daniel, I strongly recommend *The Daniel Prayer*. Anne Graham Lotz encourages believers to stand firm and never give up on God. It is within our spirits to pray and believe that the God of Daniel is the same today, according to His Word. Read this book and become a *Daniel*-like-minded believer!

Major Amir Tsarfati, Israeli Defense Force;
founder, Behold Israel Ministry

This book changed me. I will keep it open and go back to it over and over. It has transformed my prayer life. I have thrown my schedule out the window to fit *on-my-face* prayer time as the centerpiece of my every day. And this is the message for America! This is the only thing that could give us another chance. It's not too late. May King Jesus raise up at least one million warriors praying *The Daniel Prayer*.

Tom Doyle, Vice President of e3 Partners
and author of *Killing Christians—Living the
Faith Where It Is Not Safe to Believe*

If I enumerated a list of lessons I've learned as a student and spiritual daughter of Anne Graham Lotz, it would not only be long but it would be topped with the importance of intentional, passionate prayer. The incredible book you are holding in your hands is a message near and dear to Ms. Anne's heart—one she has lived and taught by example. This work will call you out of the doldrums of lackluster faith and beckon you to renewed passion for an age-old spiritual discipline that still has wonder-working power. Read it, yes, but don't stop there. Get on your knees and pray—intentionally, strategically, and fervently.

Priscilla Shirer, author of *Fervent: A Woman's
Guide to Serious, Specific and Strategic Prayer*

Also by Anne Graham Lotz

THE DANIEL PRAYER

PRAYER THAT MOVES HEAVEN
AND CHANGES NATIONS

ANNE GRAHAM LOTZ

ZONDERVAN

The Daniel Prayer
Copyright © 2016 by Anne Graham Lotz

Requests for information should be addressed to:
Zondervan, 3900 Sparks Dr. SE, Grand Rapids, Michigan 49546

ISBN 978-0-310-34544-2

International Trade Paper Edition

Published in association with the literary agency of Alive Communications, Inc., 7680 Goddard Street, Suite 200, Colorado Springs, CO 80920. www.alivecommunications.com

Cover design: Studio Gearbox
Cover photo: Comstock / Getty Images®
Interior design: Denise Froehlich

First printing March 2016 / Printed in the United States of America

To
those who long for revival

CONTENTS

*The prayer of a righteous person
is powerful and effective.*

JAMES 5:16

The air was electric.

People were shouting, crying, pleading with God. Some were standing with raised hands, others were on their knees, and still others were prostrate on the floor. My brother Franklin had just entered the auditorium, and I remember glimpsing his face at the doorway, his eyes wide as he mouthed, "What's going on?"

We were in Suva, Fiji, where Samaritan's Purse was hosting a conference for church workers. Six hundred people had come in from the dozens of surrounding islands to attend. I had just finished speaking on the prophet Samuel, presenting the tragic truth that while he was a judge, a prophet, and a kingmaker extraordinaire, Samuel was not a good father. His sons did not follow the Lord. My challenge to the mostly male audience was not to be so focused on ministry that they neglected their own wives and children.

When I issued the invitation to repent of their sin and to commit to training up their children in the Lord, almost the entire audience of pastors and church leaders surged forward. They began pouring out their hearts in an urgent, desperate, passionate pleading with God to forgive, to have mercy, to bless. They were not praying in other languages. I could understand what they were saying, but the atmosphere itself was thick with the presence of God.

I remember a woman seizing me by the arm and pulling me into her circle for prayer. *Pray?* I was totally intimidated to pray in such a group. For good reason. When I opened my mouth and tried, my voice sounded hollow. My prayer seemed wretchedly anemic in the midst of such fervent intensity.

I had never before heard prayer like I heard on that day in Suva, Fiji. Actually, rarely have I ever heard prayer like that anywhere, which has led me to wonder why our prayers often lack that kind of power, passion, and persuasion. What are we missing? What was *I missing?*

While there may be more than one answer to my question, could it be that one key ingredient that is missing is an all-out, no-holds-barred, go-for-broke, nothing-held-back, old-fashioned commitment to pray? The kind of commitment that's born out of desperation. Intense aspiration. Soulful longing. The kind of commitment athletes make to win the race or the game or the trophy or the medal. The kind of commitment that makes sacrifices, accepts responsibility, keeps obligations, and overcomes obstacles.

The kind of urgent plea we find in the Daniel Prayer.

This is not a casual, every-day, pray-as-you-feel-like-it, run-of-the-mill, garden-variety type of prayer. It is not even a flare sent up as a distress call for help. The Daniel Prayer is a commitment. A commitment that perseveres over any and every obstacle until Heaven is moved and nations are changed.

The original Daniel Prayer was a desperate plea uttered by one man, Daniel, on behalf of his nation—Judah—that had come under God's judgment. For an entire generation—for seventy years—his people were held in captivity by their enemy, the Babylonians, and separated from God's place of blessing.

The sad reality was that God had repeatedly forewarned the

nation that if there was no national repentance of sin, judgment would fall.

Daniel's people would have to have known that this was no idle warning. Because when the ten northern tribes of Israel had embraced idolatry, refusing to heed God's repeated warnings of judgment, God had sent in the Assyrians who destroyed the Northern Kingdom.[1] The Southern Kingdom of Judah, with the smaller tribe of Benjamin, was the remaining remnant of what had been the nation of Israel under King David and his successor-son, Solomon.

Now God was issuing those same warnings to Judah. He had sent messenger after messenger, including Jeremiah, Habakkuk, and Zephaniah, who had each faithfully delivered the message with every conceivable emphasis and nuance. The messengers spoke clearly, powerfully, visually, audibly, emotionally, factually, accurately, and truthfully. The people were left with no excuse and no defense for not "getting it." But the nation of Judah refused to heed God's warnings, and so judgment fell.

Judgment came in the form of the Babylonians who were ruled by the ruthless emperor Nebuchadnezzar. They had previously conquered Assyria, then Egypt. Following their conquest of those two major world powers, they swept through Judah, leveled Jerusalem, looted the temple treasures, and forcibly took God's people to Babylon in a series of three deportations, effectively enslaving the entire population. In a relatively short period of time, Judah was erased from the national scene. She no longer existed as she had for over five hundred years. She was a people and a nation in exile.

Daniel was approximately fifteen years of age when he was captured by the Babylonians and deported eight hundred miles east of Jerusalem to serve as a slave in Nebuchadnezzar's court. His situation seemed utterly hopeless and helpless. He had no human rights commission to appeal to, no friendly government to seek intervention from, no international criminal court to take up his case, no dream team of lawyers to represent him. He was abducted to serve an emperor who had absolute world power and was accountable to no one.

Yet through it all, Daniel glorified God by his character and his conduct. His service was so extraordinary that he rapidly rose up through the ranks to become a national leader as well as a counselor to kings. As young as he was, Daniel may not have known about the power of prayer from experience. But as his story unfolds, it's clear he knew something about the power of his God, although his knowledge may have been based not on his own experience, but on his nation's history. It didn't take long for Daniel, in the desperate situations he faced, to discover the power of God through prayer. Because God was all that Daniel had. Again and again he threw himself upon God with such complete faith and utter dependence that God came through for him. Powerfully. Personally. Dramatically. Repeatedly.

Daniel's meteoric rise to prominence remains even more remarkable because when he arrived in Babylon as a young teenager, he was subjected to its strange customs, unfamiliar language, elaborate dress, exotic foods, and pagan gods—a kind of cultural brainwashing. He was stripped of his identity and given a new name, Belteshazzar.[2] The purpose of the new name, which was a tribute to a Babylonian god, would have been to destroy Daniel's loyalty and allegiance to his own God. He was also cruelly stripped of his masculinity and forced to become a eunuch to make him more subservient to his new master.[3] And he was commanded to honor false gods by eating food that had been first sacrificed to them.

The cumulative message was clear. Daniel was to serve the emperor with all his heart, mind, soul, body, and strength. He was to so immerse himself in Babylon that he would be severed from his past in order to embrace the present as the only reality. Everything was designed to force Daniel to conform to the Babylonian mold to serve at Nebuchadnezzar's pleasure.

But Daniel purposed in his heart that he would not defile himself . . .[4] And thus he began his remarkable career that spanned two world empires and the entire time of his nation's captivity. At great risk to himself, again and again, he maintained his undivided devotion to God. In turn, God gave him *knowledge and skill in all literature and wisdom; and Daniel had understanding in all visions and dreams.*[5] He rose to be the equivalent of prime minister under four emperors: Nebuchadnezzar, Belshazzar, Darius, and Cyrus.

And yet Daniel never forgot the temple that had been the heart of Jerusalem and of the nation. Even at the end of his life, he remained mindful of the sacrifices that had been offered to God there as an act of obedient worship. He longed for Jerusalem every day of his life, evidenced by the fact that three times daily, when he prayed, he turned his face in the direction of his beloved city that once had been.

Again and again Daniel's life was threatened and seemed on the verge of annihilation. But each time, in response to Daniel's remarkable, steadfast faith, God demonstrated His supernatural power to honor the one who honored Him.[6] He miraculously intervened to save Daniel from Nebuchadnezzar's fury, Belshazzar's folly, and Darius' fanaticism until He performed the greatest miracle of all in answer to Daniel's prayer. God moved

Cyrus to issue the decree that after seventy years of captivity, every Jew living in Babylon could go home.

What kind of prayer was it that when offered by one person on behalf of a people who were under God's judgment, Heaven was moved and a nation was changed?[7] What was the secret to the spiritual restoration, renewal, and revival of Judah? What can we learn today from Daniel's prayer that would move Heaven and change our beloved nation? Even after a full generation of apostasy and separation from national faith in the living God, is it possible that the prayer of one person could bring renewal, restoration, and revival to America?

That's what I want to find out.

I believe it's time to pray like Daniel.

Now.

Make no mistake: our nation—and our world—are coming under the judgment of God. By the time this book is released, this reality may be even more apparent than it is now as I write. God uses dramatic world events to get people's attention. Revelation 6-19, and many other Scriptures[8], reveal that such indicators will be intertwined with His judgment in the end. The signs are all around us.

> When natural disasters—hurricanes, earthquakes, volcanic eruptions, avalanches, wildfires, floods, droughts, and tornadoes—repeatedly break records and claim lives . . .
>
> When rumors of war encircle the globe daily because mercurial leaders break treaties and shatter alliances, bully other nations, and disregard sovereign borders . . .
>
> When terrorists slaughter innocent people, creating widespread chaos and fear . . .

When our culture obsesses about celebrities without moral scruples who blatantly sensationalize their sinful exploits . . .

When women and children are trafficked and degraded for billions of dollars in pornographic profit . . .

When work, sports, movies, video games, and tech toys consume our thoughts with no time left to focus on what matters most . . .

When political solutions repeatedly fail to remedy what must begin with wet eyes, broken hearts, and bent knees . . .

It's time to look up. It's time to cry out. It's time to pray.

I realize we must be cautious when interpreting current events and natural disasters. The rain falls on the just and on the unjust. Bad things often happen to good people for no obvious reason we can discern. But God has not called me to speak tentatively or without a sound biblical basis for what I see happening around us today. There are three reasons I believe God's patience may be running out.

One: We have willingly, intentionally, deliberately taken the lives of almost 60 million children. Most of these abortions were not done for medical reasons, but for the convenience of the mother as a means of birth control.[9]

Two: Our defiance of God's institution of marriage.

Three: Our abandonment of the nation of Israel.

I use "we" and "our" to refer to our nation in these three reasons for God's judgment. Certainly, these three national sins would bring God's judgment to any group of people practicing them. But it is especially concerning to see the United States of America, a nation founded on faith in God and dedicated to His glory by our first President and the Continental Congress, defy Him, seek to remove Him from public life, and rebel against His ways.[10]

There's only one solution.

When faced with God's righteous judgment, there is nothing . . . *nothing* . . . no politics or president, no government or agreement, no institution or organization, no media or ministry, no economy or military, no alliance or treaty . . . *nothing* will turn our nation around except prayer.

Heartfelt, desperate prayer. Prayer where the pray-ers rend their hearts, return to the Cross, and repent of personal and national sin. Only prayer that moves Heaven can change a nation.

And that's the Daniel Prayer.

DANIEL 9:1–23

In the first year of Darius son of Xerxes (a Mede by descent), who was made ruler over the Babylonian kingdom—in the first year of his reign, I, Daniel, understood from the Scriptures, according to the word of the Lord given to Jeremiah the prophet, that the desolation of Jerusalem would last seventy years. So I turned to the Lord God and pleaded with him in prayer and petition, in fasting, and in sackcloth and ashes.

I prayed to the LORD my God and confessed:

"O Lord, the great and awesome God, who keeps his covenant of love with all who love him and obey his commands, we have sinned and done wrong. We have been wicked and have rebelled; we have turned away from your commands and laws. We have not listened to your servants the prophets, who spoke in your name to our kings, our princes and our fathers, and to all the people of the land.

"Lord, you are righteous, but this day we are covered with shame—the men of Judah and the people of Jerusalem and all Israel, both near and far, in all the countries where you have scattered us because of our unfaithfulness to you. O LORD, we and our kings, our princes and our ancestors are covered with shame because we have sinned against you. The Lord our God is merciful and forgiving, even though we have rebelled against him; we have not obeyed the LORD our God or kept the laws he gave us through his servants the prophets. All Israel has transgressed your law and turned away, refusing to obey you.

"Therefore the curses and sworn judgments written in the Law of Moses, the servant of God, have been poured out on us, because we have sinned against you. You have fulfilled the words spoken against us and against our rulers by bringing on us great disaster. Under the whole heaven nothing has ever been done like what has been done to Jerusalem. Just as it is written in the Law of Moses, all this disaster has come upon us, yet we have not sought the favor of the LORD our God by turning from our sins and giving attention to your truth. The LORD did not hesitate to bring the disaster upon us, for the LORD our God is righteous in everything he does; yet we have not obeyed him.

"Now, O Lord our God, who brought your people out of Egypt with a mighty hand and who made for yourself a name that endures to this day, we have sinned, we have done wrong. O Lord, in keeping with all your righteous acts, turn away your anger and your wrath from Jerusalem, your city, your holy hill. Our sins and the iniquities of our fathers have made Jerusalem and your people an object of scorn to all those around us.

"Now, our God, hear the prayers and petitions of your servant. For your sake, O Lord, look with favor on your desolate sanctuary. Give ear, O God, and hear; open your eyes and see the desolation of the city that bears your Name. We do not make requests of you because we are righteous, but because of your great mercy. O Lord, listen! O Lord, forgive! O Lord, hear and act! For your sake, O my God, do not delay, because your city and your people bear your Name."

While I was speaking and praying, confessing my sin and the sin of my people Israel and making my request to the LORD my God for his holy hill—while I was still in prayer, Gabriel, the man I had seen in the earlier vision, came to me in swift flight about the time of the evening sacrifice. He instructed me and said to me, "Daniel, I have now come to give you insight and understanding. As soon as you began to pray, an answer was given, which I have come to tell you, for you are highly esteemed."

PART ONE

PREPARING FOR PRAYER

*Devote yourselves to prayer,
being watchful and thankful.*

COLOSSIANS 4:2

COMMITTED TO PRAY

It is said that Susanna Wesley, mother to nineteen children, including John and Charles, used to throw her apron up over her face to have a few private moments for her prayers. I once heard a Bible teacher share that when her three children were small she let them run loose in the house; then she would climb into their playpen to grab a few moments of private prayer. My own mother encouraged me to "pray on the hoof"—wherever I was and in whatever I was doing. It was her paraphrase of what the apostle Paul told the Thessalonian followers of Jesus when he instructed them to "pray without ceasing."[1]

While I am well aware that we can pray anytime, anywhere, about anything, the Daniel Prayer is different. It's a commitment. And I am convinced our commitments, or lack of them, change our lives.

The most important commitment I have ever made has been to be a disciple of Jesus Christ. It has affected every area of my life, as well as every fiber of my being—mental, emotional, physical, as well as spiritual. It's a commitment that I continue to live out on a moment-by-moment, day-to-day basis. That commitment determines the way I spend my money and my time, the friends I have and the enemies I make, the habits I establish and the habits that I break, where I go and what I do. It's a commitment that has been life-altering and life-shaping.

I also made another very significant, life-altering, life-shaping commitment when I said yes to the marriage proposal offered by Danny Lotz. It led me to a milestone moment on September 2, 1966, at 8:00 in the evening. I stood in the double doorway of Gaither Chapel in Montreat, North Carolina, the small Presbyterian church in which I had been raised, baptized, and had given my first public testimony.

My hand was looped through Daddy's arm as we waited for the wedding director to give the signal that it was time to walk down the aisle. The stone chapel was packed with hundreds of special friends and guests whose heads were twisting and turning to catch a first glimpse of us. With the candlelight giving a soft, romantic feel and the profusion of white flowers giving off a subtle floral scent, the entire scene looked like something out of my dreams.

Daddy and I proceeded to walk on the same aisle cloth that he and my mother had walked over in the very same chapel where twenty-three years earlier they had been married. With my tall, eager bridegroom grinning from ear to ear ahead of us, we met him at the front of the chapel. My father kissed my cheek, placed my hand in Danny's, then stepped in front of us and led us through our wedding vows, pronouncing us man and wife. When I said, "I do," I knew there was no turning back. Because marriage is a commitment.

Now, almost fifty years later, I am still living out that commitment. It has required time. Energy. Sacrifice. It has affected me in every way, at every level, on every day. It hasn't been easy, but God has blessed our relationship. It has been challenging at times to maintain, especially when I became Danny's full-time caregiver. But I made the commitment to be his wife. I followed through on that commitment until Jesus came and took him home.[2] The duration and depth of my marriage commitment help me to understand the divine dynamic of love and sacrifice that are requirements if we are to experience God's faithfulness throughout life's mountains and valleys.

And that's the Daniel Prayer. It's a commitment to pray until the prayer is answered. It's not easy. It requires time. Energy. Sacrifice. It involves reading and pleading God's promises. It's motivated by a wholehearted love that's willing to suffer, to repent, to sacrifice—to do whatever it takes to get an answer. But whatever you have to sacrifice or invest to make the commitment, the Daniel Prayer will be worth it one hundred times over when Heaven is moved and this nation is changed.

Daniel teaches us about prayer by his own example. One thing he teaches us is that his commitment to pray required preparation. Just as an athlete can't expect to win by showing up at game time without having practiced, the commitment to pray doesn't just happen. It requires preparation.

A PREPARED PLACE FOR PRAYER

Daniel had a specific place that he designated for prayer, which was an upstairs room in his home to which he withdrew three times every day.[3] We don't know anything else about this room except that it had windows facing west. His preparations may have been as simple as setting aside this particular place for prayer where he could be undistracted and undisturbed. A refuge away from the all-consuming culture closing in around him.

I'm convinced we all need this kind of sacred space set aside for special time alone with God. My designated, prepared place for prayer in my home is the corner of my living room. On one side of the wingback chair where I sit is a fireplace. On cold winter mornings I light the fire, and it adds a cozy ambience that I find appealing. On the other side is a table with a drawer in which I keep several different translations of the Bible, three small devotional books, a Bible-study notebook, a personal journal, my reading glasses, pencil, pen, legal pad, iPad, and tissues. I want everything in place so that once I sit down to pray, I don't have to keep jumping up to find my pen or my glasses or get a tissue for my constantly dripping nose. Gathering those materials required preparation that included selecting a Bible that does not travel with me, but is used only for the purpose of prayer so that it is rarely removed from the chair side table. In that way I know it's always available when I pray.

But I also know I need the regular, disciplined prayer of others. When I began my international ministry almost thirty years ago, God impressed on my heart to establish a Personal Prayer Team. They meet on Thursday mornings in the home of one of the members. I send them a weekly prayer letter on Wednesday that lists answers to prayer from the previous week's requests, then gives more requests for the coming week. Four of the ten ladies now serving have been on my Prayer Team for the entire time. I was blessed beyond words when my daughter, Rachel-Ruth Wright, not only felt called to be on my Personal Prayer Team, but two years ago was selected to be the Chair.

While these women pray for me personally, several years ago I became acutely aware that our ministry office and staff also needed a dedicated prayer team. So I set aside a place for prayer in my ministry office. I did this when one morning in my early morning devotional study of Exodus, I was struck by the fact that

Moses had set aside a tent outside the camp of Israel and designated it for prayer. I knew God was impressing upon me to set aside a room in the office where nothing else would take place except prayer. So I did.

I selected a room in the center of the building and placed enough chairs in it for every staff person who serves at AnGeL Ministries. I had the walls painted a navy blue to give it a quiet, secluded atmosphere. At one end of the room is a small bench in front of a large cross, one made of mirrors so that those kneeling before the cross can see themselves reflected in it. At the other end of the room is an easy chair with a table beside it on which is a lamp, a box of tissues, a Bible, and a card box containing prayer requests people send to our ministry. Outside I hung a small framed sign: The Meeting Place.[4]

While the room is available for staff members to slip into during the day when they want to spend a few moments in quiet reflection, meditation, and prayer, I felt that more organized prayer was necessary. So I asked God to bring to my mind the names of women that He had chosen to be a part of the AnGeL Ministries Office Prayer Team. He did. When I called them, each one agreed to serve. Another immediate, precious personal blessing was that my daughter, Morrow Reitmeier, was one of the names God placed on my heart. She agreed to serve on the Office Prayer Team and has been a member ever since.

From that time until today, on Thursday mornings every week, these six very dedicated women gather in the Meeting Place to pray for the office staff and our ministry needs. To do so, the staff has to submit individual requests to the Prayer Chair by Tuesday afternoon so that she can email the list out to her team. That way the Prayer Team is already prepared to pray when they arrive on Thursday mornings. Once a month the Prayer Team invites a staff member to meet with them to get a fresh, firsthand grasp of his or her needs whether personal or professional.

The positive difference prayer has made in our office and ministry staff is beyond measure. My staff overflows with love for God's Word, God's Son, God's Gospel, God's people—for each other and for me. The harmony, unity, efficiency, and stability have been more than wonderful. It's been supernatural. It's clear evidence that God hears and answers prayer.

While God meets us wherever and whenever we call out to him, a Daniel-like commitment requires deliberation and preparation in order to maximize the impact of our prayers. For me, the commitment began with my decision to place prayer at the heart of my ministry, and then I have had to maintain that commitment by ensuring it is fully carried out by the Prayer Teams.

Think about this for a moment. While you may not need a team of people praying for you, do you have perhaps one or two friends who could be your prayer partners? People you could pray with once a week or when difficulties arise and you feel you need the support of someone else's prayers? And do you have a designated Meeting Place? Would you consider establishing one? Make the commitment to place prayer at the heart of your home or your office.

I understand that not everyone has the space to set aside just for prayer. When my sister's children were young and she was living in a small house, she kept her Bible study materials in a cardboard box underneath her sofa in the family room. When she had a few moments, she pulled out her box and had everything she needed for prayer. Obviously, her commitment to pray required preparing a box of readily available materials. She found a way to make it work within the context of her circumstances, something we all can do.

I know business professionals who go to their office an hour earlier in the morning to have time for prayer. Their "materials" are on electronic devices so that they have all they need to meet with the Lord before their day begins. But even electronic devices need preparation to be readily available for use in prayer. You need to have previously downloaded apps for the Bible, for devotionals, and for other materials to enrich your prayer time.[5]

Would you not only consider designating a place in your home or office for prayer, but would you make the commitment to do so? Now. Then follow through and do it.

A PREPARED TIME FOR PRAYER

Prayer helps us anchor our faith in God. It's like setting our spiritual compass so that regardless of the twists and turns during the day, the needle of our focused faith always turns to God. Daniel's life was anchored in prayer. He established the habit of meeting God in his designated place for prayer three times a day, and he maintained that commitment even when under pressure and in the face of life-threatening attack.[6]

Do you not only have a set-aside place for prayer, but a set-aside time to meet with God in prayer? When do you pray?

For years, I battled getting up early in the morning for prayer. I knew, and still know, that any time during the day is acceptable to God. But I couldn't seem to shake the conviction that early morning hours were the ideal time. The woman who taught me how to study and teach the Bible, Miss A. Wetherell Johnson, commented that when our prayer time is at night, it's like tuning our violin when the symphony is over. Because, of course, the violin needs to be tuned before the symphony so that its sound is pure. Why would we tune our instrument *after* it's been played? With the same reasoning, we need to begin our day with prayer to ensure we live in sync with God. Why would we spend time only in evening prayer after we have already stumbled through the day? While it's wonderful to end our day in prayer, she urged me to pray in the morning when the day before me was a clean slate—a blank page that had yet to be lived out.

I was also aware that again and again, a morning time of prayer is referred to in the Bible. Just in the Psalms alone there are repeated references:

> ". . . In the morning, O LORD, you hear my voice; in the morning I lay my requests before you and wait in expectation."

> ". . . I will sing of your strength; in the morning I will sing of your love . . ."

> ". . . I cry to you for help, O LORD; in the morning my prayer comes before you."

> ". . . I rise before dawn and cry for help; I have put my hope in your word."

> ". . . Let the morning bring me word of your unfailing love, for I have put my trust in you. Show me the way I should go, for to you I lift up my soul."[7]

While these examples encouraged me, the one that drew me to make a commitment to an early morning time with the Lord was not the example of David or the psalmists, but of Jesus Himself. Mark reveals that after a pressure-packed day of intense ministry, "Very early in the morning, while it was still dark, Jesus got up, left the house and went off to a solitary place, where he prayed."[8] I felt God was directing me to establish a prayer time in the morning.

But I'm not a morning person, I told myself. I'm such a sleepyhead. So although I felt drawn to get up and pray in the mornings, and although I felt convicted of disobedience when I slept to the last minute without getting up for prayer, I still didn't do it. I even had the audacity to tell the Lord that if He really wanted me to get up early, He could wake me up Himself! But I made no real decision to get up and no preparations for what I would do if He did wake me up.

There were actually times when I slept to the last minute and complained to God that He hadn't awakened me for my prayer time. Or I would wake up, but then would deliberately roll over mumbling, "God, yesterday was frantically busy, and I got to bed so late last night. I'm just too tired to get up early. I know You understand."

Yes, He did understand, but what He also understood was that I had never really made the commitment to get up for prayer and, therefore, had not followed through with the preparation for it. I had good intentions but not obedient actions.

And then God spoke to me very firmly and clearly. As I was studying and meditating on His letters to the seven churches in Revelation in order to teach them to others, He brought them home to me. Let me paraphrase His words that lovingly scalded and scolded:

> Anne, I hold you in one hand and the Holy Spirit in the other hand, like balance scales. I've weighed your life against His and you don't measure up. I know what you have been doing.

You are in ministry, traveling around the world, telling other people about Me and getting them to listen to My voice, but you are not listening to Me yourself. You have a reputation of being alive—people regard you as an exemplary Christian— but from My perspective you are falling short—spiritually dying on the inside. The prayers of your prayer team are not a substitute for your own prayers. Wake up! . . . I have not found your deeds complete in My sight because you are prayerless. Remember, therefore, what I have told you and repent.[9]

Talk about a wake-up call! I went down to the gadget store at the local mall, bought a clock that sounded like a major seven-fire alarm when it went off, and set it for thirty minutes before I usually got up to start my day. The first morning it went off, it scared me silly. My heart was thumping out of my chest, my poor husband was startled out of his wits and yelled, "What in the world is that?" and I knew there was no chance I was going to roll over and go back to sleep.

So I got up. At last I had achieved victory over those blankets in the morning! But when I calmed down, I was still sleepy as I went to pray. Yet I had made the commitment to get up for an early morning prayer time, and therefore I knew I had to make even more preparation.

This is what I came up with. After setting my alarm the night before, after bounding out of bed in the morning the moment the alarm went off, after doing my stretches on the floor to loud worship music, after walking-jogging outside for two-and-a-half miles, after getting a triple shot of espresso in my latte at the coffee house, *then* I would come back wide awake and fully engaged for my prayer time. And that worked!

It still works for me today, although I no longer need an alarm to get me up. Getting up for an early morning prayer time has become one of the joys of my life. And thirty minutes is no longer even close to being sufficient, although there are days when my obligations don't allow me to carve out any more time. When my schedule remains open, my daily time with the Lord can stretch into hours. I love it! I can't wait to meet the Lord in my designated place at the designated time. But it took a firm decision, practical preparations, and dedicated follow-through to get me to this point. Heaven-moving, nation-changing prayer requires acting on your commitment.

There is one other aspect to my preparation that I quickly learned the hard way. It's quite obvious but not always as easy to practice. If I am to get up earlier in the morning, I *must*—this is not optional—I must go to bed earlier the night before. So I do.

The time of day mattered to me for the reasons I've shared with you. But there is nothing super-spiritual about an early morning time of prayer. While every aspect of our prayer doesn't necessarily need to be uttered in one place at one time, I believe the Daniel Prayer requires a set-aside place at a dedicated time to truly be effective. You can decide the place and time that's most helpful to you for focusing on prayer. The important thing is that you follow through with a consistent commitment.

A PREPARED ATMOSPHERE FOR PRAYER

Daniel did something else that I believe helped him keep his focus when he prayed. He was surrounded by a hostile environment with enemies who were jealously trying to find an accusation they could use against him. He lived in a culture where people worshiped many gods. And while Daniel had served with distinction, the previous king, Belshazzar, haughtily referred to Daniel as one of the exiles enslaved by his father Nebuchadnezzar.[10] It was a humiliating reminder that despite the respect he garnered from his captors, Daniel was still a slave.

Three times a day, when Daniel went to his designated place for prayer, he opened his windows toward Jerusalem. The poignant gesture revealed not only the longing in his heart for his city and his people, but also his exclusive focus on the God of Abraham, Isaac, and Jacob. The God of his fathers. The God who had been with him throughout his lifetime, for over eighty years. The one, true, living God whom Daniel worshiped and served and obeyed.

While I don't open windows that look toward Jerusalem, I do look up. I look up in the direction of the New Jerusalem that the Bible calls Heaven. As I walk early in the morning and see the moon setting in the west and the sun rising in the east, I worship the Creator whose compassions never fail. His mercies are new every morning. His faithfulness never ceases.[11]

Sometimes when I see the sunrise at the beach, or the sunset over the Great Smoky Mountain Range, or see the stars studded in the night sky, I have an ache in my heart. I get homesick with longing to go Home. I am reminded that this life is not all there is.

Any difficulties we may have here are not worthy of mention when compared to the glory, honor, and blessing that He will bestow upon us when we go Home.[12] Looking up helps me to keep my focus in prayer as I'm reminded I'm communing with the great God of the universe who is in control of all things and who makes time to meet with me in prayer because He loves me. I'm important to Him. And so are you.

You don't have to look out your window or look up. There are a variety of ways to prepare the atmosphere for your prayer time.

Once in a while, change your designated place to one that's outside where you can reflect on the beauty of His creation. Or use the words of hymns or praise songs to help you stay focused. You can play praise-and-worship music to create an atmosphere that helps you transition from your daily routine into God's presence. You can even use aspects of color and décor to set the mood in the space you've set aside. Just consider what will help you focus on God.

Daniel prepared an atmosphere that was conducive to helping him stay focused in prayer by opening his windows toward Jerusalem. He transcended his captivity and escaped into God's presence, bending down on his knees while looking up with his heart.[13]

A PREPARED ATTITUDE FOR PRAYER

Daniel's body language helped him remember as he prayed that he, Daniel, a slave in exile, had an audience with the One who is the living God, All Glorious, Most Holy, the Ancient of Days, the Almighty. The One who had put His Name on Jerusalem forever. The One who had declared that His eyes and His heart would always be there.[14] The One who would never forsake His people even when they were in exile.[15] When Daniel bowed his knees to God, it was an outward gesture that revealed his inner attitude of humility, reverence, submission, and allegiance to the One so much greater than himself or any earthly king or world ruler.

When was the last time you prayed on your knees? Have you ever prayed on your knees? Try it. The difference your outward position makes in your inner attitude as you pray may surprise you.

Daniel not only prayed from a kneeling position, but he made a habit of giving thanks to God. He cultivated an "attitude of gratitude"—of thanksgiving despite circumstances that were less than ideal. Think about it. His enemies were lurking outside his window plotting his death. He was over eighty years old and still enslaved eight hundred miles from home. He served a ruthless king who had destroyed his beloved city and butchered countless people, many of whom I'm sure Daniel had known and loved. His boyhood dreams had faded. At this stage of his life, he must have also come to the rude awakening that he would never go home. He would never see his beloved Jerusalem again. And *still* he was thankful. How could that be?

What about you?

When life throws you a curveball, are you thankful?

When your expectations, goals, and dreams have not been realized, and never will be, are you thankful?

When your life's circumstances go from bad to worse, are you thankful?

When your critics are watching every move you make, anxious to catch you in something they can use to discredit you, are you thankful?

When you are enslaved by a body of pain, or an abusive spouse, or a demanding employer, or an uncaring parent, are you thankful?

How can anyone be thankful in those circumstances?

Daniel's attitude illustrates one of the great secrets of trusting God. The key to thankfulness is not to view God through the lens of our circumstances, but to view our circumstances through the lens of God's love and sovereign purpose. God had called Daniel not to a life of comfort and ease, but to a life of greatness.

And so Daniel could thank God for everything in his life. He knew, as he entered his winter years, that all things had worked together for his good to enable him to fulfill God's purpose.[16]

As a result, Daniel did indeed live a life of greatness. Perhaps from Heaven's perspective, there is in fact no greater prophet in the Old Testament than Daniel. We are still referring to his prophecies to make sense of what we see happening in our world today.

Despite his circumstances, Daniel's faithfulness to God also distinguished him among those around him. With God's favor, he rose quickly through the Babylonian system so that he stood out with exceptional distinction among the many other exiles captured from Judah. During his lifetime, he served as a counselor to the king, as a provincial governor in Babylon, then as prime minister under Nebuchadnezzar, Belshazzar (for one night), Darius, and Cyrus. And his knowledge of astronomy is still acknowledged today as having influenced the wise men who, approximately five hundred years later, traveled from the east to worship the newborn King of the Jews in Bethlehem.[17]

Simply put, Daniel was remarkable.

If he had given in to self-pity, anger, resentment, bitterness, unforgiveness, or a vengeful spirit with a "why me?" attitude toward God, I doubt we would ever have heard of him. Instead, three times a day, every day, Daniel found reasons to be thankful.

What is your attitude? Especially when you're in "captivity"— bound in some way that restricts what you want to do or where you want to go or who you want to be or what you want to have. When God has allowed you to be in some sort of exile—cut off from friends, family, that which is familiar; when He has denied you personal wealth, health, prosperity, happiness—are you thankful to Him?

I wonder . . . will you settle for just getting by as a follower of Jesus, or do you aspire to greatness? Don't settle for less than fulfilling completely the potential that God had in mind for you when He brought you into existence, then brought you to Himself in a personal relationship. Yield your life to God's purpose even when it may seem the very opposite of anything you may have thought you had wanted. While God's purpose may be radically different than the plan you had laid out for your life, make no mistake about it, His plan is much greater and broader . . . it's more lasting and impactful . . . than any plan you could come up with for yourself. I know . . . from personal experience. And so did Daniel.

COMPELLED TO PRAY

Growing up in the Montreat Presbyterian Church taught me a lot about prayer. From the time I was born until the time I married and moved away from my parents' home, I was a member of this small congregation tucked into a mountain valley. We met in an old stone college chapel in the Blue Ridge Mountains of western North Carolina. The membership was comprised primarily of retired missionaries, each one of whom could share firsthand experiences of the power of prayer. It was the congregation my maternal grandparents joined on their return after twenty-five years on the mission field in China. Although my parents were married there and my mother was a member, my father never joined the church. I'm not sure how Mother and Daddy worked things out, but my mother remained a lifelong Presbyterian and refused to become a Baptist. My father to this day is a lifelong Baptist and has refused to become a Presbyterian.

I loved that little church and still do. It's where I was baptized, where I gave my first public testimony, and where I was married. One of my earliest memories in church was of Dr. Fogarty, who pastored there when I was a little girl. I'm not sure if he was old at the time or just seemed old to me because I was a child, but he made a vivid impression. He wore a long, black flowing robe that billowed out behind him when he walked down the aisle. I could feel the air moving in his wake even when my eyes were closed because, after the benediction, while the choir sang a brief postlude, he would dash to the back of the chapel to greet people as they left.

But his pastoral prayers are what stand out in my memory. With all due respect, he prayed forever! When he bowed his head to pray, I took that as my cue to take a nap. I would put my head on my grandmother's soft shoulder and drift off. It was easy to fall asleep when Dr. Fogarty prayed because his fluid voice was so singsongy. And his lullaby tone of prayer seemed to go on and on and on. To this day, when someone prays in that professional, languorous, almost TV-announcer voice, it requires great effort for me not to tune out and drift off.

Recalling those childhood memories, I now wonder what my prayers sound like to others. What about yours? Have you ever prayed simply because it was expected of you? Maybe you were in a group at church, and perish the thought, they prayed around the circle and you had no way of getting out of it. And if you're like most people, myself included, the entire time others were praying, you were preoccupied with what in the world you were going to say when it was your turn.

It can be daunting to pray in public, particularly when we aren't expecting to be called upon to do so. Consequently, I wonder if we get conditioned to pray in certain ways about certain things just to be polite and fit in. It's the equivalent of saying "just fine" when someone asks you how you're doing. You may be as far from fine as possible, but that's what just seems to come out by default.

So Christians learn to pray in certain ways because that's what good Christian people do, right? We pray for our children. We pray for our friends. We pray for our church. We pray for our nation. We pray that God would bless the missionaries and all the children in Africa. And we feel pretty good about ourselves for doing so. We feel even better about ourselves if we can pray out loud in public without stuttering.

The Daniel Prayer is dramatically different from these kinds of prayers. Instead of socially conditioned small talk, the Daniel Prayer is a 911 call for urgent help. The Daniel Prayer is storming the gates of Heaven with what Eugene Peterson calls "reversed thunder"—praying God's Word back to Him. It's prayer that penetrates Heaven and impacts a nation. There is nothing professional or formulaic about it. It is passionate, heartfelt, laser-focused, soul-gripping, I-won't-let-You-go-until-You-bless-me, pleading-until-you-get-an-answer kind of prayer.

When was the last time you heard someone pray like that? When was the last time you heard someone pray to the point that you became more aware of the One to whom the person was speaking, than you were of the person doing the speaking? When was the last time *you* prayed like that? Think about it. What is the key to that kind of praying? *Is there a secret?*

The answers lie in the Daniel Prayer itself. Daniel's plea not only reflects a serious commitment, but it's a prayer that's prayed under compulsion. It's a prayer that is born deep within your soul and erupts up through your heart until it pours out on your lips in an unself-conscious flow of words that are infused with the Spirit of God until it almost quivers with a spiritual electricity.

COMPELLED BY PROBLEMS IN OUR WORLD

Daniel's prayer pulsates with this type of emotional conviction. As we have already seen, his life for sixty-seven years had been difficult at best. Now, as an old man, he lived through another violent regime change as the Medo-Persian Empire overthrew the

Babylonians. His position was precarious and uncertain under the new ruler. He may have felt an increasing apprehension about the security of his people's future. At the very least, he was living in an unsettled, rapidly changing world.

The problems in his world are implied by the brief statement, "In the first year of Darius son of Xerxes (a Mede by descent), who was made ruler over the Babylonian kingdom . . ." (9:1). But rather than wring his hands and roll his eyes, Daniel opened up his copy of the Scriptures to see what God had to say about his world's situation. In the end, it was the combination of the problems in his world and the promises in God's Word that ignited a fire in his heart, compelling him to give voice to his prayer.

Because the Daniel Prayer is not an everyday type of prayer. It's a prayer birthed under pressure, squeezing the coal of our heartache, grief, and desperation into the diamond of genuine faith that pleases God, moves Heaven, and changes nations. It can be triggered by a disappointment or a sudden revelation of hope, an unanswered prayer or a promise freshly received, the consequences of a past failure or a miracle that lies just over the horizon. It's a plea for something you intensely long for that you know will take place, but has not taken place yet.

To be honest, every time I pray I am not gripped by that kind of intensity and compulsion. Sometimes, however, there was no other way I could pray.

> When I struggled with infertility, longed to get pregnant, but month after month, did not . . .
>
> When I was confined to a small home with small children and yet deeply desired to serve the Lord in full-time ministry . . .

When the door of service was opened and I found myself in the pulpit looking at five hundred upturned, expectant faces waiting to hear what I was going to say . . .

When I have stood on the platform in a soccer field in India, a racetrack in Australia, a prison auditorium in North Carolina, the General Assembly of the United Nations, a tent in Northern Ireland, the funeral service for my mother, and many, many other places where I felt way in over my head . . .

When I sat in the hospital chapel with the family of my close friend who was being taken off life support after a sudden twenty-four-hour virus . . .

When I overheard my son and his first wife in a heated argument that signaled the beginning of the end of their marriage . . .

When I returned home with my three children after having been gone for two hours and found the front door broken down and everything of value in the house taken by thieves . . .

When I discovered my seventy-eight year old husband to whom I had been married for almost forty-nine years in our pool, unresponsive . . .

On occasions like these, and on many others, simple, memorized now-I-lay-me-down-to-sleep types of prayer just won't do. A prayer that's mechanical or perfunctory doesn't come close to communicating what's in my heart.

But the Daniel Prayer is not just venting to God or yelling at Heaven. The Daniel Prayer is not just an outpouring of heartfelt emotion and passionate pleading. It is an outpouring of heartfelt emotion and passionate pleading based on God's Word as we hold Him to His promises.

COMPELLED BY THE PROMISES IN GOD'S WORD

For example, in each of the situations I gave above, God had given me a promise, and it was His promise that was the basis for my prayer . . .

When I struggled with infertility, longed to get pregnant, but month after month did not, God promised me in 1 Samuel 1:17 that He would grant what I had asked of Him. In answer to prayer, He kept His word. In time, I not only gave birth to a son, but to two daughters.

When I was confined to a small home with small children and deeply desired to serve the Lord, He revealed from Hosea 2:14 that He had intentionally placed me in the "wilderness" so that He could speak to me and I would learn to listen to His voice. His Word was true. I did not waste my wilderness years, but studied the Scriptures, and thus was prepared when He called me out to teach the Bible to others.

When the door of service was opened and I found myself in the pulpit looking at five hundred upturned, expectant faces waiting to hear what I was going to say, He clearly confirmed my call in Jeremiah 1:4–7 to go wherever He sent me and to say whatever He commanded me. Although my timidity and shyness caused me to be physically sick before I spoke for the first six weeks of teaching, I remembered His word that I was "not to be afraid of their faces" and so did not give in to the fear.

When I have stood on the platform in a soccer field in India, a racetrack in Australia, a prison auditorium in North Carolina, the General Assembly of the United Nations, the funeral service for my mother, and many, many other places where I was in over my head, He assured me from John 3:34 that He would give me His Spirit without limit. I have now experienced His promised sufficiency for more than forty years as He has always been faithful to equip, enable, and empower me to be fully obedient to His call.

When I had been upbraided by the interpreters during my briefing before speaking at the 1983 International Congress for Itinerant Evangelists in Amsterdam who did not think I was up to the task of addressing 5,000 world church leaders, or working through the 150-plus interpreters who would be communicating my message to the evangelists in front of me, God reassured me from 1 John 2:27 that I had received an anointing from Him, so I was not to worry. Because I was still quaking in my shoes, knees knocking, feeling very faint (and that was during the preparation time, *before* I stepped up on the platform), God reassured me again from Psalm 133:2 that the anointing was so full the message was saturated in it. He was again true to His word. As evidenced by the demand for the audio version, my message at Amsterdam '83 ranks second only to my father's among all the many gifted speakers there. Because "in me is no good thing"[1] and "without Him I can do nothing,"[2] I humbly acknowledge and am deeply convinced that the message was exceptionally well received only because God chose to bless it and fulfill His promises to me.

When I sat in the hospital chapel with the family of my dear friend who was being taken off life support after a sudden twenty-four-hour virus, He conveyed to me His anger over the temporary victory death seemed to have, but immediately reminded me from John 11:25 and 40 that He is the resurrection and the life, and that if I just believed Him, I would glimpse His glory. He kept His word. I did glimpse His glory when I was given the privilege of speaking to the hundreds of people who gathered for my friend's funeral service, and many responded by putting their trust in Jesus.

When I overheard my son and his first wife in a heated argument that signaled the beginning of the end of their marriage, He acknowledged my emotional turmoil, yet lifted the veil briefly through Isaiah 54:10–13 so that I caught a reflection of His glory in the future of my family. While there is still more yet to come, I have already seen each member of my family reflect the glory of God in the most unexpected ways.

When I returned home with my three children after having been gone for two hours and found the front door broken down and everything of value in the house taken by thieves, He reminded me from Matthew 6:20 that my real treasures were safely in Heaven. I have reminded myself of His promise on many occasions. While I enjoy material things, I have learned to hold them loosely as I know by firsthand experience that the real treasure is what's inside of me.

When I discovered my seventy-eight-year-old husband, to whom I had been married for forty-nine years, in our pool, unresponsive, I jumped into the water, pulled his head up on my lap, and prayed the Daniel Prayer as passionately . . . as desperately . . . as I ever have. I readily recalled a promise memorized in childhood: "God is our refuge and strength, an ever present help in trouble. Therefore we will not fear."[3] God quickly brought emergency responders to our aid. They were able to restart

Danny's heart. As I followed Danny to the ER and then into ICU, I did not fear. I had complete peace that was like a river deep within. It was peace "which surpasses all understanding."[4] It really wasn't logical considering what I was going through. Two days later, with my precious children and their spouses surrounding Danny's bed, I gave permission to the hospital medical team to remove him from life support. They did, and with a flood of tears running down our faces, we sang to him, read Scripture to him, and praised the God of Heaven who is always good, loving, faithful . . . and who knows best. As Danny took his last breath, I claimed out loud the promises in Revelation 21 and 22 . . .

Now the dwelling of God is with [Danny], and He will live with [him]. [Danny] will be His people, and God Himself will be with [him] and wipe every tear from [his] eyes. There will be no more death or mourning or crying or pain, for the old order of things has passed away. . . . I am making everything new! . . . These words are trustworthy and true. . . . To [Danny] who is thirsty I will give to drink without cost from the spring of the water of life. . . . The throne of God and of the Lamb will be in the city, and His servant [Danny] will serve Him. [Danny] will see His face, and His name will be on Danny's forehead . . . and [he] will reign forever and ever. . . . These words are trustworthy and true. . . . Behold, I am coming soon!"

I knew that Danny had passed from death to real life. He was in the presence of his Lord and Savior. He was finally Home. And I will see him again.

Later, my inner peace was challenged as I agonized in reflection on what to me seemed like an horrific accident. God directed me to Isaiah 25:1 . . . "O Lord, you are my God; I will exalt you and praise your name, for in perfect faithfulness you have done marvelous things, things planned long ago." And I knew, and know to this day, that my husband's death was not an accident. It was God's foreordained time for him to move to Our Father's House. And so my heart has been filled not only with peace, but with praise for His perfect faithfulness to carry out to completion what He had begun in Danny's life seventy-eight years ago.[5] Danny had finished his race.[6]

I have learned by experience that prayer which moves Heaven is a commitment to pray that is confirmed by God's Word, while the compulsion to pray is often triggered by our problems.

We have already touched on the fact that Daniel, who was in his eighties, having lived in captivity as a slave for sixty-seven years, was no stranger to problems. Personal, professional, spiritual, relational, or national, he experienced them all to a greater or lesser degree. But Daniel also knew what it was to open up the Scriptures and pray according to the promises he found in God's Word. Which is impressive to me. Who would think that this old man, having lived as a slave in captivity for sixty-seven years, would still be reading the equivalent of his Bible? But he was. He reveals that "I, Daniel, understood from the Scriptures, according to the word of the LORD given to Jeremiah the prophet, that the desolation of Jerusalem would last seventy years" (9:2).[7]

As Daniel poured over the Scriptures, he came across a verse that seemed to be illuminated. God drew Daniel's attention to a verse that had been there all along, but one that was filled with fresh meaning for him on that particular day as God spoke to him through it. It was the promise he discovered during his Bible reading in Jeremiah that gave Daniel insight in how to pray for his people. Yet it was more than just insightful information. It was a promise Daniel proceeded to claim personally on behalf of his people.

PROMISES THAT ARE PERSONAL

God still speaks to us personally through His Word. The morning I wrote this chapter, I was reading my *Daily Light,* a small volume I have read since my mother gave me my first copy at ten years of age.[8] It consists of a compilation of Scriptures for both morning and evening. As I read the morning portion, verse after verse "leaped up off the page," and I knew God was speaking to me. Let me explain.

I had just been in prayer, telling the Lord that I wasn't sure how much longer I could continue caring for my husband while overseeing my ministry, and then adding the writing of this book to an already full schedule. My husband's caregiving not only kept me close to home, but it became increasingly challenging because of his very fragile physical condition, his progressive mental confusion, and his wide emotional swings. But this is how the Lord spoke to me in response to my heart's cry. Listen and see if you can overhear His voice: *Be strong . . . and work; for I am with you . . . Be strong in the Lord and in the power of His might . . . Let your hands be strong, you who have been hearing in these days these words by the mouth of the prophets* [Daniel] *. . . Go in this might of yours . . . Therefore, since* [you] *have this ministry, as* [you] *have received mercy,* [you] *do not lose heart . . .* [Don't] *grow weary while doing good, for in due season* [you] *shall reap if* [you] *do not lose heart.*[9]

What encouragement that gave me! What a total lift to my spirit! And I knew God was giving me insight, not so much in how to pray for others, but how to pray for myself.

God speaks personally to us through His Word, but we need to learn to listen to His voice.[10] One way to listen is to pray before you read your Bible. Talk to God about what's on your heart and mind. Then open His Word and "listen" with your eyes on the page. He may not speak to you every time you read it, but He will speak.

You and I will never know how to pray in such a way that Heaven is moved and our nation is changed until we start reading our Bibles. A dramatic example of this is found in Genesis 6 when God clearly and emphatically said He was going to destroy the world because it was so permeated with sin, evil, and wickedness. Although He issued the warning, only one person in the entire world seemed to be listening: Noah. A man who was not only right with his neighbors, but right with God. And Noah made time to walk with God, indicating a personal relationship that involved interactive communication.

One day when he was walking, God spoke to Noah, revealing what was on His mind: judgment. He was going to destroy the world and every living thing in it. But then He also revealed what else was on His mind: salvation from judgment. And He told Noah specifically what to do about it. He was to build an ark as a means of salvation for the human race and the animal kingdom. Noah claimed God's promise of salvation by doing everything exactly as God said. As a result he, his family, and the human race were saved.[11]

Abraham was another man who walked with God. As he did, God shared with Abraham His intention of destroying Sodom and Gomorrah. Abraham was deeply concerned because his nephew Lot lived in Sodom. So Abraham began to intercede for Sodom, asking God to spare it for the sake of the righteous who lived there. God did not find enough righteous people living in Sodom to justify delaying or withholding judgment. But when He destroyed the cities, He went out of His way to save Lot and his family in answer to Abraham's intense, persistent prayer.[12]

When you and I pray the Daniel Prayer, pleading with God according to His Word, someone else's salvation, like Abraham's nephew Lot, may depend on it. So how do you read your Bible? Do you read it to increase your knowledge of the facts and information only? Or do you read it listening expectantly for God to speak to you, then talk to Him about what He has said, basing your prayers on it? Start the habit of reading your Bible each day and highlighting promises or phrases that you can use as the basis of your prayers for our world, for our nation, for others on your prayer list, as well as for yourself.

It's a habit that was held by two of the women whom God used to help shape my life. One was Miss A. Wetherell Johnson, the founder and director of Bible Study Fellowship. She taught and trained me to teach the Bible with accuracy, with balance, and with a heart of passionate love for the Author as well as the audience.

My last conversation with her was on the phone. I knew, unless God miraculously intervened, that she would soon lose her battle with cancer and move to Our Father's House. I wanted to call her but didn't want to intrude. I didn't know what I would say. But I wanted desperately to hear her voice one more time. So I got up the courage and called. To this day, I'm embarrassed to admit that when I heard her weakened, rather high-pitched English accented voice, I became emotional and blurted out the most ridiculous thing I could have said: "Miss Johnson, how are you?"

Remarkably, she understood my heart and didn't address my painfully obvious question. As she proceeded to answer, I knew I would never forget what she said. She told me she spent her days just trying to overcome the pain while she thanked God for medication. Then she said, "I've just been reading the life of Jacob once again and I learned . . ." Her voice trailed off and I didn't catch what she had learned! Sensing her fatigue, I couldn't bear to ask her to repeat herself. But what I learned is that at the end of her life, she was still reading her Bible and learning new things!

The other woman whose love for God's Word greatly impacted my life was my own mother. Indelibly impressed on my mind is the picture of Mother toward the end of her life as she sat on her bed, unable to walk or get around easily because of arthritic pain in her back and her hips. She was arrayed in her white flowing dressing gown, long pearls looped around her neck, white hair like a halo about her head, eyes sparkling as her hands held her big black Bible. The fire was crackling on the hearth, and she was surrounded by pages that had two inch tall words typed on them. Because of her macular degeneration, she could no longer read the Bible that she still held in her hands with such love. But she was memorizing Scripture that her assistant had typed out for her in large block letters. She was excited to tell me she was memorizing Romans 8 and what she was learning from it.

Both Miss Johnson and my mother were in their eighties—the same age Daniel was when he recorded his prayer. No wonder all three of them prayed in such a way that Heaven was moved and nations were changed.[13] Their prayers emerged and blossomed from the depths of God's Word. If our prayers are not rooted in what God has said, what is their basis? A wish? Or a want? Or a hope-so?

For some people, prayer merely expresses their wishes or wants to God. To be candid, it's perfectly acceptable for you and me to tell God what we want or hope for. He knows anyway, and sometimes it just helps to talk it out with Him. For instance, when I was talking to God about the challenges I am currently dealing with, telling Him that I wanted relief from stress and pressure, His response was to say clearly, "Anne, be strong." He also gave me the key to strength on that same page in the *Daily Light* when He said, "I am the vine, you are the branches. He who abides in Me, and I in him, bears much fruit; for without Me you can do nothing."[14]

It wasn't exactly what I wanted to hear at the time, but it was the answer. And it changed the way I prayed. Instead of praying, *God, give me a break,* I began praying, *Lord, I choose to be strong in You as I abide in total dependency upon You through prayer, Bible reading, and obedient faith. One day at a time I will go forward in Your strength. Thank You for supplying all that I need.*

Do you see the difference? Prayer that moves Heaven and changes a nation, as well as changes your life and mine, is prayer that is based on God's Word. If you have a specific need, want, wish, or hope, put it in the form of a request, then open your Bible and ask God to speak to you about it. He may change the way you are praying, as He did with me. Or He may confirm the way you are praying.

Ask Him for a promise on which you can base your prayer. A promise for your children, your spouse, your parents, your career, your church, your health, your finances, our nation or our world, or whatever is uppermost on your mind. Then pray. God loves to be held to His Word. I'm continually encouraged by the ways He consistently demonstrates His faithfulness to it.

For instance, just as I was reviewing this section of the manuscript, my daughter Rachel-Ruth called. While she is our youngest child in years, she is extremely mature in her spirit. I have watched in amazement as God has uniquely gifted her in three primary ways: One, as a mother. Two, as a Bible teacher. And three, as a woman of prayer who, for lack of a better description, is a see-er. Someone who sees into the spiritual world, and who knows how to gain victory over the enemy in dramatic ways.

As Rachel-Ruth's voice came over the phone, it was almost husky, breathless, and I could tell she was holding back her emotions. Then, as she told me how God had just spoken to her, I understood why. She shared that as she was fixing breakfast for her three girls, she had turned on the television news and was reminded that one year previous to the day, 276 Nigerian girls had been kidnapped by the terrorist group, Boko Haram. After she had driven her children to school, she had come back to the house and had opened her Bible to work on the message she was going to give to her class. Her message was about Paul's experience of getting swept up into a dangerous, life-threatening storm that resulted in a shipwreck. Her eye fell on Acts 27:37, which reports that, "Altogether there were 276 of us on board," then in verse 44, "everyone reached land in safety."

To Rachel-Ruth's consternation and amazement, the number of kidnapped girls matched exactly the same number of those whose lives were endangered on Paul's ship during the storm at sea. Using this "divine coincidence" as a catalyst, she immediately felt that God in Heaven was alerting her to pray for the girls. Which she did right away. And although I knew she had already prayed, we prayed together over the phone for the girls that we knew had Heaven's undivided attention at that moment. And we will continue to pray until all 276 are safely home, either with their parents in Nigeria, or with their Heavenly Father.

Did our prayers for the Nigerian girls move Heaven? We don't know yet. As of this writing, we are not aware of any change in their circumstances. *But the answer is not our responsibility.* When God burdens us with what burdens Him, our responsibility is to pray. Then we leave the answer up to Him. And who knows? Across the ocean, deep in the heart of Africa, back in the jungle were the girls comforted with a sudden awareness of God's love and His presence? Did they have a flash of hope as they knew inexplicably that they were not forgotten? That they were on God's mind and He would deliver them one day and bring them Home? Were they given the strength to make it through one more day? Because when Rachel-Ruth was alerted, she paid attention and prayed.

While you and I may not have as dramatic a word from the Lord as Rachel-Ruth seemed to have regarding the Nigerian girls, the principle is the same. God speaks to us through His Word, and it's His Word that we need to "speak" back to Him in prayer.

PROMISES THAT ARE CONDITIONAL

God's Word gives strength to our feeble prayers, doesn't it? Which is one reason why the Daniel Prayer is so powerful. It flowed from God's Word. The promise that Daniel came across in his Bible reading was Jeremiah 29:10–14 . . .

"This is what the LORD says: 'When seventy years are completed for Babylon, I will come to you and fulfill my gracious promise to bring you back to this place. For I know the plans I have for you,' declares the LORD, 'plans to prosper you and not to harm you, plans to give you hope and a future. Then you will call upon me and come and pray to me and I will listen to you.

You will seek me and find me when you seek me with all your heart. I will be found by you,' declares the LORD, 'and will bring you back from captivity. I will gather you from all the nations and places where I have banished you,' declares the LORD, 'and will bring you back to the place from which I carried you into exile.'"

When Daniel read those verses, I wonder if he rubbed his eyes, then reread them. Did his heart skip a beat and his breath come in short snatches? Maybe he had a quick intake of breath, holding it until he quickly calculated how long he had been in captivity. Sixty-seven years! Three years less than the seventy God had said would be the duration of the exile! Did that mean that in three years the captives would be set free? Did that mean that in three years they would all be going home? *Back to Jerusalem?* Would the long night of captivity soon be over?

He must surely have been thrilled beyond words by this incredible thought. It was almost too good to be true! But then . . . Was there a small whisper in his heart? Just a brief thought that was struggling to come to the forefront of his mind. Did he pursue the thought and go back to reread Jeremiah, this time not looking for the promises, but for any conditions that needed to be met in order to receive those promises? There they were! Right there in black and white . . . *Then you will call upon me and come and pray to me and I will listen to you. You will seek me and find me when you seek me with all your heart.*

With his mind racing, did he wonder who else was reading Jeremiah? Who would call upon the Lord? Who would come to Him in prayer? Who would seek Him with all of their hearts on behalf of the nation in exile? God had spoken to His people through Daniel's contemporary, the prophet Ezekiel, putting

them on notice that while He had promised certain things
to them, He was waiting for those promises to be claimed
in prayer before He fulfilled them.[15] So I wonder . . . in that
same moment, did the light of truth break through, and did
Daniel know that, whether or not anyone else was praying for
and claiming God's promise of deliverance, he would? And if
he was the only one praying, what difference would it make?
Daniel was going to find out.

One promise for our nation that has been prayed frequently
comes from 2 Chronicles 7:13–15. If a promise could be worn
out from use, this one might be tattered beyond recognition.
But promises cannot be worn out. They are just as valid today
as when they were first issued. They are like gold. They don't
even tarnish. In fact, the more we claim them, the more they
seem to "glow" with even greater meaning. Then why has
this one not made more of a difference in our nation? Could
it be that while we eagerly claim the promise of God hearing
our prayer and forgiving our sin and healing our land, we have
given little attention to the condition attached to it? And what
is the condition? We must humble ourselves. Pray. Seek God's
face. *And turn from our wicked ways.*

What difference would it make if we claimed this promise
while also meeting the condition for receiving it? Like Daniel,
I want to find out. So with the condition in mind, let's take a
moment and pray 2 Chronicles 7:13–15 together:

> *Lord of mercy, God of grace, hear us as we pray. You
> have promised that when environmental disasters
> erupt, or the enemy strikes, or illnesses break out,
> that if we . . . Your people who call ourselves by Your*

name . . . the Church . . . Christ-followers . . . if we
would set aside our pride and self-righteousness and
judgmental finger-pointing, make the time to get alone
with You and pray, seeking not just a political solution
but Your face, turning from our own grievous sin, then
Heaven would be moved! Sin would be forgiven! Hearts
would be changed! And you would bless our land!

So now we humbly confess to You our sin of
_____, and _____, and _____. We name it
for what it is in Your sight, and choose to put it out of our
lives. Out of our minds. Out of our hearts. To turn away
from it. We ask You to cleanse us with the blood of Your
Son and our Savior. Hear our prayer. Forgive us our sin.

Now, we ask, please. Open Your eyes to our beloved
nation. Answer us according to Your Word, for the glory
of Your Name. Amen.

3

CENTERED IN PRAYER

Having been raised in the Blue Ridge Mountains
of western North Carolina, I have always loved to hike. When I
was young, every Sunday afternoon my entire family, including
one or more dogs, would hike to the ridge behind our home.
I loved the woodsy smell of the leaves as I scuffed my shoes
through them. I loved the roaring sound that grew louder the
closer we got to the ridge where there was no barrier to break
the fierce intensity of the wind. I loved looking for box turtles
half submerged in the muddy runoff of the springs beside the old
logging road.

When we made it to the end of the road, we hiked the last
several hundred feet on a trail choked with underbrush that
required we walk single file. To make sure I was going in the
right direction, I had to keep my eyes on Daddy, who always
went first. I knew if I kept my eyes centered on him, eventually
I would come out to the bare place on top of the mountain that
Mother had named the Reed Field, where we could see all the
way down the Swannanoa Valley to Asheville. I learned early in
life that it's necessary to have a center point when hiking in thick
woods. Daddy was my center point.

This lesson was confirmed when I was a teenager on a
fourteen-mile hike with a friend. Starting out behind my

home, we climbed to the top of the mountain known as Little Piney Ridge, then hiked the ridgelines of the Seven Sisters to Greybeard. The path my friend had chosen was not marked, so we just kept to the highest points along the mountain range. We knew eventually we would come out to the trail that led up to Greybeard, where a spectacular view of multiple states awaited us.

About an hour before we reached our destination, we got lost in a laurel thicket. While that may sound humorous, it wasn't. Laurel bushes are low, thick, and they can cover the side of a mountain. It's impossible to see out of them in any direction. So my friend pulled out a compass. She adjusted it so that the needle pointed north, then motioned for me to follow her. As she kept her eye on the compass, we fought our way through the bushes. North was our center point. As long as we kept the needle on the compass pointed in that direction, we were able to hike to a place where we could get a better perspective of where we were and subsequently found the trail we were looking for. Eventually we made it successfully to the top of Greybeard.

You and I need a center point when we pray. Our faith needs to be focused on the One to whom we are praying or it really isn't a prayer. This fundamental truth was pinpointed in a tweet sent out by a Japanese freelance journalist who reported live from Syria. His heart-wrenching words September 7, 2010 went viral: "Closing my eyes and holding still. It's the end if I get mad or scream. It's close to a prayer. Hate is not for humans. Judgment lies with God. That's what I learned from my Arabic brothers and sisters."[1] His emotional and meaningful words were "close to a prayer," but in his own estimation fell short because they were not focused on Anyone. He didn't have a center point.

PRAYER IS LIFE'S COMPASS

If prayer is our compass in life, then the needle that points north is the focus of our faith in prayer on the living God. He is the "north" on our "compass." He is the Center-point. When our prayers are focused, regardless of what life throws at us, whether it's a long, hard climb to the top of our profession or career, or the steady trail of perseverance as we set out to achieve our goals, or the confusion and lost feeling that can envelop us when we find ourselves in a thicket of problems and pressures and pain—if our prayers are focused on the living God, they will make a difference. In us. In our circumstances. In others. In our church. In our nation. In our world.

One key reason that the Daniel Prayer moved Heaven and changed nations was because Daniel's faith was centered on the living God. Before Daniel even gives us the words of his prayer, he makes it clear that he "turned to the Lord God" (9:3). He set his compass.

Focusing on God as my True North helps me see beyond my temporary circumstances here on earth and reminds me of His unchanging character as well. Years ago, I adopted the habit of beginning virtually every prayer I pray with worship. As I center down on the One to whom I'm speaking, I try to think of the specific attributes of His character that would be relevant to my prayer. For instance, if I'm burdened for my children, I address Him as my Heavenly Father, worshiping Him as a parent who is supremely patient, loving, good, yet has children that are not perfect. He understands parental agony and heartbreak.

If I'm hurt and wounded, I address Him as the One who was wounded for my transgressions, bruised for my iniquities, who understands the feelings of my pain, and who has promised to heal my broken heart. If I have just been blessed or honored, I address Him as the Fountainhead of all blessing, the Giver of every good thing. If I am coming to Him aware I've sinned, before even confessing it to Him, I worship Him as the God of mercy and grace who loves sinners, who is never surprised by my failure because that's all He expects of me in my flesh, who stands ready to pardon and cleanse all those who come to Him by faith at the foot of the Cross.

It's amazing how the simple exercise of putting my focus on who God is helps put my prayer into perspective. My problems don't seem so overwhelming. My questions don't seem so critical. My worries don't seem so all-consuming. My fears don't seem so paralyzing. Centering down on Him brings peace and calmness to my spirit. In the quietness very often I hear His whisper as He directs me out of the current "laurel thicket."

On the other hand, if I begin my prayer focusing . . .

> on the doctor's grim prognosis for my loved one,
>
> or on the probability of a conflict with my child's teacher,
>
> or on the impact of the company's downsizing my job,
>
> or on the seemingly nonstop environmental disasters in our nation,
>
> or on the increasing prevalence of active shooters,
>
> or on the raw savagery of radical militant jihadists,

. . . I become overwhelmed to the point that I have no faith whatsoever that my prayer will make any difference at all. The outcome of my focus makes my worries and fears appear to be inevitable. The enemy just seems too powerful. The result? I develop a nauseous knot in the pit of my stomach, and I get lost emotionally and spiritually in the laurel thicket.

When do you set your compass? Do you turn to others before you turn to the Lord God? The Daniel Prayer has helped me refocus on the priority of centering down when I talk with God. And centering down requires privacy, an attitude of undistracted attention focused singularly and intimately on who God is and on my conversation with Him.

PRIVACY MATTERS WHEN WE PRAY

When Daniel turned to God, it's implied that he turned away from everyone and everything else so that he could pray privately. The effectiveness of private prayer is dramatically illustrated by a beautiful Old Testament story. Elisha, the prophet who succeeded Elijah in ministry, was himself ministered to by a well-to-do woman and her husband. Whenever he was in the area, he would stop by their home to have a meal with them. The woman set aside a guest room that she made available for him when he needed a place of retreat to rest. Out of gratitude, he inquired what he could do for her. He was informed that she was barren. He promised her that she would have a son within the year. She did!

When the boy was old enough to go out into the field with his father at harvest time, he suddenly complained of a severe headache. He was carried to the house where he died of an apparent sunstroke. Elisha was called. "When Elisha reached the house, there was the boy lying dead on his couch. [Elisha] went in, shut the door on the two of them and prayed to the LORD." Elisha needed seclusion so that he could pray freely without distraction—without the doubts, fears, tears, and emotions of the parents or anyone else.

God heard and answered Elisha's private prayer. As Elisha prayed, the boy's body grew warm. He sneezed seven times, then opened his eyes! Elisha called for the woman, and she received her son who had been brought back to life![2]

Jesus Himself, when summoned by the ruler of the synagogue whose daughter had become severely ill, went to the man's house. But by the time He arrived, the little girl had already died. Jesus put everyone out of the house, took her by the hand, and she got up! She was raised to life.[3]

Privacy in prayer matters.

Jesus emphasized privacy in prayer to His disciples in the Sermon on the Mount, "When you pray, go into your room, close the door and pray to your Father, who is unseen."[4] Then He set a personal example of repeatedly seeking His Father in private prayer: "Jesus often withdrew to lonely places and prayed."[5]

Privacy in prayer not only matters, I think it's essential. Especially if we are going to pray the Daniel Prayer. We must be alone with God, isolated from all props of human reason or help. It's when we are removed from the doubts or suggestions or grief or criticism or comments of others that we vault into the "vast blue inter-stellar space"[6] where we hang on God alone and get in touch with the fountain of miracles. If we want to pray in such a way that Heaven is moved and nations are changed, we must have a secret prayer chamber. We must detach ourselves from outward distractions and attach ourselves inwardly to the Lord alone if we are to receive the fullness of His answers.

I know for myself that I can't seem to concentrate in prayer when someone else is moving about in my house. Even if that person is not in the room with me, just knowing they are up and about is distracting to my spirit. One reason I get up so early in the morning to pray is because I need privacy. I seem to require early morning stillness, before others stir or the phone rings, in order to enter into communion with God.

It's been said that the pious, religious hypocrite needs an audience to pray because he prays to be heard.[7] To impress. But Jesus told His disciples not to be like the hypocrites. Instead, He instructed them "when you pray, go into your room, close the door and pray to your Father, who is unseen. Then your Father, who sees what is done in secret, will reward you."[8] Jesus was affirming that privacy matters in prayer. He set the example for us again and again as the Bible tells us . . .

"He withdrew . . . privately to a solitary place."

"Jesus often withdrew to lonely places and prayed."

"Jesus went out to a mountainside to pray, and spent the night praying to God."

"Jesus was praying in private."[9]

There is no denying that when Jesus prayed, Heaven was moved and the world was changed. Which leads me to wonder, if you only pray when you are with others or you are in church, how effective and active is your prayer life? Isn't it time for you to draw aside? To turn away from anything and everything, anyone and everyone, to make the time to get alone with God? Because privacy in prayer matters.

Luke's Gospel tells us that Jesus took three of His disciples— Peter, James, and John—up a high mountain. While they were there alone, as He was praying, His appearance drastically changed. His clothes became dazzling white—as brilliant as a flash of lightning. His face shone with the brilliance of the sun. And the light was not being reflected from anything. The light was coming from within Jesus. The disciples were seeing Him transfigured in His glory as Son of God—the glory that He had laid aside when He had become the Son of Man.[10] What an unforgettable experience of private prayer that must have been! But what followed is a lesson that God has driven down deep into my heart.

When Jesus and the three disciples went back down the mountain into the valley, they were met by a small riot. People were arguing with each other and with the religious leaders. When Jesus inquired what was going on, a man stepped out from the mob. He explained that he had brought his son who was totally out of control to Jesus' disciples for help. But they had been unable to help him. Jesus rebuked His disciples for their lack of faith, then He healed the boy. Later, when His disciples asked Him why they had been unable to help, Jesus replied, "This kind can come out by nothing but prayer and fasting."[11] To paraphrase His words, He was impressing on His disciples that to tap into Heaven's power, they needed to pray . . . turn to God. And fast . . . turn away from everything else.

The lesson God drove home to me was this: Had Jesus invited all twelve of His disciples to draw aside with Him for a time of private prayer? Did only three of them accept His invitation? Did the other nine give excuses such as: "I don't have time," "My family needs me this weekend," "I'm too busy in ministry," "Climbing that mountain is hard work—I'm too tired," "I've got other things to do"?

For whatever reason, the critical truth is that the nine who had not made the effort to draw aside and spend time in private prayer with Jesus on the mountain had no power to help others in the valley. And so I have asked myself, *If my prayer doesn't move Heaven or change nations, could it be that I have not spent time on the mountain with Jesus—in private prayer?* What about you?

Our modern life is not conducive to private prayer, is it? If your days are like mine, they're full to the brim. I stay on the go from early morning until I crash in bed at night. Each one filled with the tyranny of the urgent . . . meals and medical appointments and medicines, phone calls and emails and voicemails, cleaning and washing and cooking, meetings and speaking and supervising. If I waited until I had the time to draw aside and pray, I doubt I would ever pray. So I have to make the time for private prayer.

To be honest, I'm afraid not to make the time. I don't want to miss out on the power that's necessary to really help others. I don't want to miss out on the power that's necessary to impact the world around me. I don't want to miss out on the power of prayer that moves Heaven and changes nations. But I will miss out if I don't make the time to draw aside with Him in private prayer.

While I know that I can pray any time and any place, in the midst of everyone and everything, in front of thousands or in a circle of dozens, I also know that privacy matters. There are times I need to be alone, free of distractions and interruptions. Just by myself with my Heavenly Father.

SINCERITY MATTERS WHEN WE PRAY

Forsaking everything to make the time to get alone with God and pray is a form of fasting. *Fasting* simply means to go without anything and everything to make time to pray. We associate it most often with abstaining from food, but it can also be abstinence from business, emails, phone calls, ministry, entertainment, web surfing, meetings, housework, shopping, cooking, talking, television, technology—the list is unlimited. While in prayer we *turn to* God, in fasting we *turn away* from everything else.

One reason we fast is not to show God how pious we are. He already knows. It is not a "work" we are to add to our prayer effort to merit His answer. His answers are gifts of His grace, not rewards for our work. It is not to make God love us more or pay us more attention. He loves us completely, fully. He can't love us any more. And He has already given us His undivided attention without our fasting. So why do we fast?

One reason is because Jesus expects us to fast. He told His disciples, "*When* you fast . . ."[12] Not *if* you fast. For myself, fasting has helped to purify my motives in prayer. It sharpens my focus on Heavenly things and clarifies my perspective on earthly things. It prompts me to pray more persistently and frequently. And perhaps most importantly, it reveals how sincere I really am as I seek the Lord in prayer.

Have you ever fasted from anything? The Daniel Prayer is a prayer of utmost, personal, passionate sincerity. It requires fasting. Daniel "turned to the Lord God and pleaded with him . . . in fasting . . ." I suggest you start to build fasting into your prayer life, if you haven't already. Talk to God about it, then decide what you will fast from, when you will fast from it, and how long you will maintain your fast. Then do it. Discover for yourself the difference it makes.

I first discovered the power of fasting when my husband, Danny, and I were newly married. We enjoyed just being together for a while, but then came the day when we decided we wanted children. In my naïveté I thought all I had to do was to stop using birth control and babies would start coming. I was wrong. Month after month, my womb would empty out. I went to specialists who assured me nothing was wrong, but they couldn't tell me why I did not get pregnant.

I shared my grief with my very wise mother, who responded, "Anne, if more mothers prayed for their babies like Hannah prayed for hers, maybe we would have more Samuels." So I turned in my Bible and read about Hannah to learn what was so unique about her prayer life.[13]

I discovered that she was greatly beloved by her husband, whose only words of comfort to her were that she ought to consider him better to her than ten sons. But a husband—even a loving husband—was no substitute for a baby. She knew that, and so did I. Hannah wanted her own baby with such intensity that she wept and could no longer eat. She fasted from food. Then she fasted from everything when she went up to the temple to pray.

In answer to her prayer and fasting, God promised her a son. Soon after, she became pregnant and gave birth to Samuel, a little boy that she dedicated to God. Samuel grew "in stature and in favor with the LORD and with men,"[14] becoming an exceedingly great man who was a prophet, judge, and kingmaker in Israel.

Following Hannah's example, I set aside one day each week to pray and fast for a son. One year after I turned to the Lord with deep sincerity on a regular, weekly basis, I seemed to hear God whispering to my heart, *Anne, you don't have to fast anymore. I will give you a baby. You will have a son.* I immediately stopped fasting and praying, and instead, started praising God for having heard and answered my prayer. The next month, I conceived a baby. Nine months later I gave birth to our son, Jonathan.

Was I able to get pregnant and give birth to Jonathan because I had fasted? I honestly don't know. What I do know is that fasting changed me. By the end of that year of prayer and fasting, I was genuinely, sincerely satisfied with the Lord and with my husband. If I had not gotten pregnant, if I had never had any children at all, I knew I would be okay. Interestingly, it was when I let go and released my desire for a baby that I became pregnant. So, indirectly, fasting seemed to play a significant role, because without it I don't believe I would have been able to release my all-consuming passionate desire for a child.

NECESSITY MATTERS WHEN WE PRAY

Privacy and sincerity certainly matter to God when we pray. And He also honors our crying out to Him when we have no one else to turn to and nowhere else to go. When we feel there is no other person who can understand our pain, God is there for us.

When have you been in such a hard place, you were desperate? When have you had no one to turn to? No doctor or lawyer, no friend or family member, no priest or pastor, no boss or business colleague. No one that you could call for help. To be all alone in your world can be a very vulnerable and terrifying place.

Daniel was desperate. He not only fasted, but he dressed "in sackcloth" (9:3), a humble garment made of woven remnants or perhaps goat hair or camel hair. No linens or silks or brocades or even cottons. Clothes that the poorest of the poor wore, signifying outwardly his inward desperation. By his very appearance, he was saying, "God, I need You. If You don't answer my prayer and keep Your promise, I have no hope. There is no one else I can turn to. My hope is in You, and in You alone."

No pretense or pride, no indifference or independence, no self-reliance or self-righteousness, no Plan B if this didn't work

out. There was no foreign aid to ask for, no stronger nation
to appeal to, no international court to hear his grievances, no
friendly military to stage a coup, no hope whatsoever anywhere
in the world. Daniel was desperate on behalf of his people. God
was his only hope. If God didn't deliver his people from captivity,
they would not be delivered. If God did not restore them to the
place of His blessing, they would not be restored. If God didn't
draw them back to faith in Himself, they would never experience spiritual and national revival. In the Daniel Prayer, necessity
matters.

Necessity also mattered to Dori, a woman caught up in the
turmoil of the Syrian civil war. She was desperate.[15] She had been
the privileged, almost spoiled wife of a wealthy Syrian busi-
nessman. She had lived in Damascus, shopped in Europe, and
vacationed in Dubai. But then one night she had received a phone
call from her brother-in-law telling her that her husband had just
been arrested and that she had to immediately flee her home with
her two teenage children. With tears streaming down their faces
as they glanced back at their palatial home, they crept through the
shadows of the night as they began their sixty-five-mile journey
on foot to safety.

About five days later they found themselves in a holding camp
two miles short of the Syrian-Jordanian border. With no food.
No running water. No toilets. On the second night in the camp,
with her starving children shielding her movements from any
casual observer, Dori dug under the fence, walked to the highway, and began flagging down the passing trucks, begging for
food and water. Four times trucks stopped, but the drivers were
only interested in getting something from Dori, not giving anything to her. The fourth time she fought off a would-be rapist,

another trucker saw what was happening and stopped to help. Warning her of the extreme dangers of begging on the highway, he graciously and generously gave her food and water. When she thanked him effusively, the Syrian man said, *The Lord Jesus bless you, Dori. Look to Him. He will be your shelter.* Then he was gone. Dori had no idea what the man was talking about, but she felt a strange peace come into her heart as she took the food back to her children.

The next day Dori and her children climbed under the fence and crossed the border, walking two more days to Amman. With the little bit of money she had brought with her, she was able to secure an old, rundown apartment in the center of the city. She was helped by a kind woman who described herself as one of the "Bible people." This woman, named Samar, not only helped Dori and the two young people get settled in the apartment, but she explained to Dori who Jesus was when He began appearing to Dori in her dreams. Finally, Dori made the dangerous decision to leave Islam and follow Him, knowing that her choice could cost her life.

Several nights later, as Dori lay on the cold, hard cement floor, listening to her daughter's soft weeping and her son's grumbling, she decided to pray. Without doubt, Dori had never heard of Daniel, but she prayed the Daniel Prayer out of desperation. *Jesus, we are so tired and hungry. We have nothing in this apartment. It's a miserable life, but I know You love us . . .* then she drifted off to sleep.

The next morning as sunlight poured through the only window in the apartment, she was startled awake by an insistent knock at her door. Apprehensive, she rose to answer, but her son got to the door first and opened it. A delivery man stood at the door with his arms filled with groceries. When Dori inquired who sent him, he replied he didn't know because he had lost the list of refugees. But he asked her if she needed food. When she nodded affirmatively, he handed her the groceries as he explained that someone in the alley had pointed him to her apartment. Then he was gone.

But first thing every morning that week, she heard a knock at her door. When she opened it, she would find a delivery man. Never the same man, always different. And each one brought different things. One brought more food. Another brought clothes. Then beds and blankets. Coats and jackets. Space heaters. At the end of the week, Dori's apartment was furnished and her refrigerator was full.

Because necessity matters to God.

HUMILITY MATTERS WHEN WE PRAY

Dori's story reminds me that the Daniel Prayer doesn't have to be fancy or long or filled with Bible verses. In fact, I almost wonder if it needs words at all. It really is a heart's cry, isn't it? But one that is uttered sincerely, in private, and out of necessity. And one wrapped in complete humility.

Recently, I spoke at a Christian gathering that was multigenerational, multiracial, and multidenominational. Before I spoke, a young pastor walked up to the platform to lead in prayer. Then he prayed. With eyes wide open, walking back and forth, gesturing to the congregation, he didn't miss a beat as he "prayed."

He was smooth, dynamic, polished, articulate . . . and proud? I hesitate to say that because only God could see his heart, but he came across as being almost spiritually arrogant. Haughty. There was no humility in his words, body language, or gestures. He seemed to be performing to impress instead of praying. And he certainly didn't lead me into God's presence. In fact, the spirit within me recoiled. His "prayer" reminded me of a story Jesus told to those "who were confident of their own righteousness and looked down on everybody else."[16]

In the story, or parable, Jesus describes two men who went up to the temple to pray.[17] One was a Pharisee, a highly educated leader in Israel who was so scrupulous in the way he kept all the nuances, regulations, and traditions of his religion that he was considered exemplary. The other was a tax collector who was considered a "low-life" because, although a Jew, he collaborated with the occupying Romans for pay. Most tax collectors were also cheats and were despised by "good" people as sinners.

So Jesus described these two men from God's perspective. The Pharisee "stood up and prayed about himself," saying, "God, I thank you that I am not like other men—or even like this tax collector. I fast twice a week and give a tenth of all I get." Then Jesus contrasted the Pharisee with His description of the tax collector who "stood at a distance. He would not even look up to heaven, but beat his breast and said, 'God, have mercy on me, a sinner.'"

In the event that someone listening didn't understand His meaning, Jesus summarized His story, "I tell you that this man [the tax collector], rather than the other [the Pharisee], went home justified before God. For everyone who exalts himself will be humbled, and he who humbles himself will be exalted." Because God doesn't just listen to our words when we pray. He evaluates our attitude in prayer. He's not impressed at all with our reputation . . . who we think we are or who others think we are.

He looks on the heart. In case there is any doubt, Proverbs clearly states, "The LORD detests all the proud of heart."[18] On the other hand, God confirms, "This is the one I esteem: he who is humble and contrite in spirit, and trembles at my word."[19]

In other words, someone like Daniel. As we have already seen, he had entered Babylon as a slave. While he remained a slave all of his life, he had quickly risen through the ranks of officials in Nebuchadnezzar's court until he was ruler over Babylon.[20] Daniel held this high position under three more emperors in three successive empires: Belshazzar who briefly ruled in Babylon, Darius who destroyed the Babylonians and ushered in the Medo-Persian Empire, and finally Cyrus who eliminated the Medes and set up the Persian Empire. In anyone and everyone's estimation, Daniel was a very great, important, powerful man.

Daniel was lavishly honored by kings for his almost unlimited, supernatural wisdom. God revealed to Daniel the dreams of others, as well as what the dreams meant. Angels personally delivered God's answers to Daniel's prayers. And God had miraculously delivered him when his enemies had contrived to have him fed to lions. It was obvious that he was a very great, important, powerful man in Heaven's estimation too.

Daniel was also a prophet in the Old Testament who is considered the equivalent to the apostle John in the New Testament. The 100 percent historical accuracy of his predictions has been phenomenal. For this reason, his insight into the world from his day until the end of time is still endlessly studied by scholars and theologians who consider him to be a great man by modern standards.

Daniel, whose greatness bridged world empires and transcends the centuries, who had every human "right" to think highly of himself, didn't. As he began to pray, he smeared himself with "ashes" (9:3). He humbled himself. Because he knew humility matters to God.

It's interesting how pride can creep into our attitude when we pray, isn't it? We think if we keep all the "rules," if we're good, moral, helpful, thoughtful, then somehow God owes us the answer we want. So after prayer, when our spouse walks out on us, or the doctor diagnoses us with a terminal illness, or a business partner betrays us, or our home is robbed, or our child is abused, then we angrily feel God has somehow let us down. And we become offended with Him.

When Danny and I first got married, we lived in a university town. Every Sunday night, we opened our home to student athletes for fellowship, Bible study, and prayer. Some were on football scholarship, while others were on the basketball and lacrosse teams. In addition we had two cheerleaders. Danny and I loved them all. And they loved us. I would fix a homemade pie or cake, and we would sit around eating the desserts and discussing the Scriptures.

I'll never forget a football player who came into our home one Sunday night very dejected. He was a huge offensive lineman. His team had played an archrival the day before. They had taken the football all the way down the field in the fourth quarter. The last play was fourth down with less than one yard to the goal line. His coach had decided not to go for a field goal, because the three points would not have been enough to win the game. They needed the six points a touchdown would give them. They would go for the touchdown.

Sitting in our small living room, the tough lineman's face reflected what then happened. He said as they broke the huddle, he had prayed to God, asking His help to power the ball over the goal line so his team could score the winning touchdown. He lined up for the play, the ball was snapped, but the opposing team had held them. They had not been able to get the ball into the end zone. So they had lost the game. Between bites of his apple pie, the big football player hung his head and, with a dark look, shared that he felt God had let him down on the one-yard line. We all tried to talk him through it, but he never came back to our home. To this day, Danny and I have grieved over him.

If you are honest, would you say you are like the big lineman? Do you think God has let you down in some way? Could it be that there is pride lurking like a cobweb in the dark inner recesses of your heart? Pride that suggests God owes you something. That you deserve better. That you deserve anything. Maybe it's time you smeared yourself with ashes.

Daniel was compelled to pray by the problems he saw in his world, and the promises he had read in God's Word. He had a laser-like focus centered on the Lord. So in the privacy of his upstairs room, with his window opened to Jerusalem,[21] he began to plead with God in utmost sincerity, out of desperate necessity, and with deep, genuine humility.

And that's where the Daniel Prayer begins . . .

PART TWO

PLEADING IN PRAYER

*Rend your heart
and not your garments.
Return to the L*ORD *your God,
for he is gracious and compassionate,
slow to anger and abounding in love,
and he relents from sending calamity.
Who knows? He may turn and have pity
and leave behind a blessing.*

JOEL 2:13–14

PLEADING WITH CONFIDENCE

It was my privilege to serve on a panel that discussed *Patterns of Evidence for the Exodus*, a documentary released nationwide with great success. In response to a question posed by the moderator, Gretchen Carlson, the Reverend Jonathan Morris, who, along with Gretchen is a regular contributor to FOX News, remarked that faith was a gift that he was grateful God had given him. I mentally . . . and silently . . . processed that comment for a few moments.

Is faith a gift that some people have been given and others have not? I knew if I had the opportunity to address what I felt could lead to a misunderstanding, I needed to take it. A few moments later, I was able to emphasize that faith is a choice.

It reminds me of an old story, a favorite of mine, about the veteran tightrope walker who, after demonstrating he could push a wheelbarrow filled with sand across Niagara Falls on a tightrope and the people applauded his stunning ability, asked for a volunteer. No one in the spectating crowd moved. Finally, a little old man in the back raised his hand, stepped forward, and offered, "I've seen what you've done, and I've heard what you've said. I believe you can push me across, so I'll do it."

Everyone in the crowd held their breath and strained to watch as the wheelbarrow was rolled over the falls . . . and back again. On the final return, the roar of the crowd was deafening as the old man emerged from the wheelbarrow. The acrobat gallantly bowed, saluted, smiled broadly, and said, "Thank you, sir, for your faith in me."

The point of the story, of course, is that while everyone in the crowd had said they believed the tightrope walker *could* carry a man across the falls in his wheelbarrow, only the little old man demonstrated real faith by climbing into the wheelbarrow. Real faith is more than just words or rituals or going to church or having a religion or believing there is a God. Real faith backs up words with actions or it's not real faith.[1] Like exercising a spiritual muscle, real faith grows as we make choice after choice after choice.

CONFIDENT FAITH IS DEVELOPED BY CHOICES

My first real choice of faith was made when I was a girl of eight or nine years of age. After watching a film on television portraying the life of Christ, I chose to confess to God in prayer that I knew I was a sinner, that I was sorry, and that I claimed the death of Jesus Christ on the Cross as His sacrifice for my sin. I asked Him to forgive me, then invited Jesus to come into my heart and life.

This choice led to opening my Bible and making the choice to read it on a daily basis. I remember reading the Bible all the way through by the time I was nine years old. Besides strengthening my small seedling of faith, it began my lifelong love affair with the Scriptures.

That choice led to the next one that stands out in my memory. It was a choice I made several years later, when I was about fifteen years of age. I was with a group of friends listening to a guest speaker in the chapel of the church where I was raised. We were attending a meeting for the youth of the church on a summer Saturday morning, and the speaker was a distinguished professor of divinity at Yale University. All of us were interested in hearing what he had to say.

I can't remember what began to alarm me about what he was saying, but I do remember when he said that there was a god for the Old Testament and another god for the New Testament, and a different god for today, my heart pounded out of my chest. Without thinking, I jumped to my feet, interrupted him, and said that was not what the Bible said. In an extremely condescending voice modulated to intimidate me, he inquired, "And just what do you think the Bible says?" Quickly, to my mind, God brought these words, "The Bible says that Jesus Christ is the same yesterday, today, and forever."[2] He had a startled, somewhat offended yet quizzical look on his face, as if to say, "Who has dared to challenge me?" But an all-out confrontation was avoided because my friends pulled on my shirt, "Anne! Sit down! He's a professor from Yale, for goodness' sake. Be quiet!" So I sat down. But while I may have been silent on the outside, I was still arguing on the inside.

About two years after I had confronted the Yale professor, I made a life-defining choice of faith when I knelt down by the window seat in my bedroom and surrendered my life for service to Jesus Christ, a decision that I continue to live out on a daily basis. Thus began a lifetime of choices, some small, some large, some public, some private, but each one seemed to build on the next one, serving to strengthen and develop and grow my faith until . . .

. . . I was able to step onto the platform of an international congress, face ten thousand evangelists in front of me with the who's who of the evangelical world seated behind me, and confidently proclaim the words God had given me.

. . . I was able to place my unresponsive husband on an EMS gurney, command the responders to stand still for a moment while I prayed, then put him in the ambulance confident his life was in God's hands and God would take care of him.

. . . I was able to confront the president of the United States publicly when he misquoted the Scripture as saying "the beginning of wisdom is toleration of others." I felt like I was fifteen years old all over again, yet this time there were no friends to pull me down. Just the East Room of the White House filled with religious leaders who were so silent you could hear a pin drop as I took four minutes to explain that the Bible says the beginning of wisdom is fear of God.[3]

. . . I was able to stand in the podium of the United Nations General Assembly and present the Gospel as the only way to have genuine, permanent world peace. And then to finish my prepared three-minute remarks even after the mic was turned off on me.

I could not have confronted the president nor addressed the United Nations gathering when I was fifteen years old. Or even fifteen years before I was given that opportunity. While I understand that God has enabled some Christians to grow up very quickly in their faith, God has graciously allowed my faith to develop over a lifetime of choices.

While you may not have the luxury of a lifetime ahead of you to make the critical choices that will develop your faith, it's important that you start. One choice at a time. God knows how long you will have to develop your faith and He will make sure that it's sufficient. But you must start.

Daniel is Exhibit A of a man who demonstrated real faith through choice after choice after choice. He not only said he believed, but he backed up his words with death-defying actions, which were not as spectacular as the acrobat crossing Niagara Falls but were equally phenomenal. We are not told when he originally made his choice to believe, but all indications are that it was during his early years growing up in Jerusalem.

By the time he walked on the stage of world history as a teenager, his faith seemed remarkably well developed, but still required him to make choices. Some of his choices are worth considering in more detail, not only because they reveal the growth of his faith, but because they give us an understanding of the way he begins the Daniel Prayer.

Daniel's first choice recorded in Scripture is one that took place after what could only be described as the horrific day when the Babylonian troops surrounded Jerusalem, then conquered it. They proceeded to search out the cream of the intelligent, gifted, personable, handsome, capable young men, enslaving them and transporting them back to Babylon to serve in King Nebuchadnezzar's court. Daniel and three of his friends— Meshach, Shadrach, and Abednego—were caught up in what is known as the first deportation from Jerusalem to Babylon of approximately two hundred young men.

When Daniel arrived in Babylon, he was immediately plunged into an intense three-year brainwashing regimen. In an effort to uproot him from his past and remold him according to Nebuchadnezzar's pleasure, Daniel was stripped of his Hebrew name, which meant "God is my judge." The new name assigned to him, Belteshazzar, was intended to give him a Babylonian identity, one paying tribute to a pagan Babylonian god. It was an unveiled effort to destroy Daniel's faith in his own God.

At the same time, more than likely, he was also stripped of his masculinity, since his immediate supervisor was described as the "master of [the] eunuchs," implying Daniel was one (1:3 NKJV). This was surely intended to force Daniel into a subservient position of humiliation, which underscored that his only purpose in life was to serve Babylon. It was made painfully clear to him from the beginning that he would have no personal life at all. He lived to serve Nebuchadnezzar.

While it was impossible for Daniel to prevent the changing of his name or his emasculation, he drew the line at being forced to eat the king's food that had first been sacrificed to idols. While he knew, of course, that the idolatrous ritual in no way changed the food, Daniel also knew to eat the food offered to idols was an indirect way of giving tribute to them. Because Daniel's faith was centered on the living God of Abraham, Isaac, and Jacob, to give tribute to other gods, even indirectly, would be to betray and deny his own God. So he "resolved not to defile himself with the royal food and wine, and he asked the chief official for permission not to defile himself this way" (1:8).

THE CHOICE TO BE FEARLESS

The choice to make that request, as innocent and reasonable as it sounds to you and me, was actually death-defying. It was the equivalent of climbing into the wheelbarrow and being pushed over Niagara Falls. Daniel put his life on the line. Ashpenaz, the chief eunuch, immediately recognized it for what it was and reacted strongly. Although he personally liked Daniel, he explained that the king himself had assigned the food and to reject it in order to have a substitute diet was to place all of their lives in grave danger. Daniel could so easily have told God, *Well, I tried. You know in my heart I'm not giving tribute to these gods, but I have to survive.* And then eaten the king's food that was placed before him.

But Daniel did not back down. Not even a little. He had made the choice not to defile himself. So the only alternative he could think of was to place his life in God's hands. Since Ashpenaz, as the chief official, had already denied his request, Daniel went to his guard and suggested a test. He asked the guard to serve him and his three friends a different diet that would be free of the association with pagan gods. Then, after ten days, if he and his friends were not better off than the other young captives who ate the king's food, the guard could do whatever he chose. Which implied the guard could execute them all for insubordination if it didn't "work."

God honored Daniel's trust and moved the guard to agree. Ten days later when they were evaluated, Daniel, Meshach, Shadrach, and Abednego "looked healthier and better nourished than any of the young men who ate the royal food" (1:15). They remained on that diet, and three years later, when the king himself gave them their final exams, they were found to be ten times better than all their advisors and professors.

Daniel had in reality put God to the test. God came through for him in such a way that Daniel's faith was surely strengthened and grew. Which was a very good thing, because within a short period of time, he made another confident and death-defying choice of faith when King Nebuchadnezzar had a series of deeply disturbing dreams.

When the king awoke from his bad dream, he called in all of his counselors, demanding that they tell him his dream and what it meant. His astounded counselors declared they couldn't possibly give him the interpretation of the dream unless they were first told what the dream was. But the king knew if he told them his dream, they could make up the interpretation. On the other hand, if they told him his dream without any prior knowledge of it, they would be demonstrating real wisdom so that more than likely their interpretation also would be valid. So the enraged king was adamant that the wise men should be able to discern what his dream had been and then tell him what it meant.

Even when he threatened to cut them into pieces and turn their houses into piles of rubble if they did not do what he demanded, the terrified astrologers knew they could not do what the king required. Death was staring them in the face. Surely with wide-eyed horror in their eyes, knees turned to jelly, hearts melted within and heads that spun dizzily, they must have gasped as they gave their emphatic answer. "There is not a man on earth who can do what the king asks!"(2:10).

Furiously, the king ordered their execution. What good were wise men if they couldn't answer his question and meet his need? And that led him to conclude that wise men generally were good for nothing, so that in his rage he decreed that all the wise men in Babylon were also to be executed. And because that was Daniel's category of service it meant that he and his three friends had just been given a death sentence.

Under orders from the king, the military commander came to arrest Daniel and carry out the execution. Daniel did not run. He did not try to escape. He did not organize a band of rebels and revolt against such irrational injustice. Instead, Daniel respectfully inquired why. When the commander explained, Daniel requested an audience with the king, asking for time to consider the matter.

The king's lingering fear over what his dream could mean must have overruled his rage, and he agreed. While everyone's life hung in the balance, Daniel asked his three friends to pray for him. Once again, with his confidence surely bolstered by his earlier experience of God's faithfulness regarding his diet, Daniel made the choice to "climb into the wheelbarrow." He put his faith in the living God and acted on it. And once again, God came through.

THE CHOICE TO BE FAITHFUL

How could Daniel possibly have gone to sleep with so much riding on his ability to discern and interpret Nebuchadnezzar's dream? If he was indeed given the king's dream during his own sleep, then that in itself was miraculous! However God gave it to him, he had the dream and the interpretation by the morning light. Daniel's thrilling, soaring confidence in God, as well as his emotional relief, punctuated his morning prayer in heartfelt, overflowing thanksgiving:

"Praise be to the name of God for ever and ever; wisdom and power are his. He changes times and seasons; he sets up kings and deposes them. He gives wisdom to the wise and knowledge to the discerning. He reveals deep and hidden things; he knows what lies in darkness, and light dwells with him. I thank and praise you, O God of my fathers: You have given me wisdom and power, you have made known to me what we asked of you, you have made known to us the dream of the king" (2:20–23).

When Daniel went to the king, Nebuchadnezzar's eyes must have narrowed as he looked skeptically at this young Israelite slave, asking, "Are you able to tell me what I saw in my dream and interpret it?"(2:26). Daniel's fearless answer reveals his rocklike confidence in God when he replied, "No wise man, enchanter, magician or diviner can explain to the king the mystery he has asked about, but there is a God in heaven who reveals mysteries. He has shown King Nebuchadnezzar what will happen in days to come" (2:27–28). Then Daniel proceeded to describe the dream and its meaning.

The king was astounded! He confirmed Daniel had accurately described his dream; therefore, the interpretation must also be accurate. And it was. More significantly, God was glorified as the king acknowledged that Daniel's God is the God of gods and the Lord of kings. And Daniel was honored by being made ruler over all of Babylon.

Daniel's faith grew more and more confident each time he made the choice to exercise it. The strength of his faith prepared him for the next choice we are told about, when the Bible records he was ushered into the drunken feast of King Nebuchadnezzar's spoiled successor, Belshazzar. During Belshazzar's feast, a mysterious hand without an arm had appeared and written something on the wall that no one could interpret. The king suddenly went stone cold sober and terrified, shaking uncontrollably from limb to limb.

Remembering Daniel's unique ability to interpret mysteries, the queen mother told the king to send for him. What a contrast with all the wealthy, spoiled, drunken, baffled officials Daniel must have made with his dignity and humility. He would have been an old man with the deep etchings in his face of godly character, and a fearlessness in his eyes that would have made the king shudder in his miserable spirit. Although the king addressed Daniel with disrespectful, condescending words, Daniel didn't hesitate or even flinch. He unleashed the full warning of God's judgment because of the king's arrogant, willful, and wicked ways that "did not honor the God who holds in his hand your life and all your ways" (5:23). Even as Daniel spoke, the Medes and Persians slipped under the gate of the city, and by morning, Belshazzar was dead and his kingdom had passed to Darius.

It was during the reign of Darius that Daniel was given another dramatic opportunity to climb into the wheelbarrow. He made a choice that demonstrated his faith not only to those in his world, but a choice that has been retold and talked about in every generation since.

THE CHOICE TO STAY FOCUSED

The choice perhaps more than any other that seems to sum up Daniel's confident faith was made when Darius appointed Daniel as one of his three top officials. But Daniel was so exceptional that Darius planned to make him second in command over the entire kingdom. The other rulers were jealous and began a private investigation of Daniel in the hopes of coming up with something they could smear him with and so prevent his promotion by discrediting him in the eyes of the king. They found nothing, except that three times a day Daniel went into his upstairs room, opened his window toward Jerusalem, and prayed. But his prayer life was enough to give them ammunition against him. They seized it.

The rulers went to Darius with smooth, flattering words, and convinced him to issue a decree that people could only pray to him and to no other god. The obviously egotistical Darius agreed. Being fed to starving lions would be the penalty for disobedience. The horror of such a death would surely be a strong deterrent against centering on any god besides Darius.

Daniel was aware of the decree, but again he didn't flinch. There was not a stutter in his step as he climbed to his upstairs room. He did not even close his shutters so that he could pray unobserved. Instead, as always, he opened his window toward Jerusalem and continued praying three times a day. Sure enough, his enemies were lurking in the shadows. They saw him in prayer and ran gleefully to report to the king.

The king was genuinely distressed because Daniel held great favor in his estimation. His eyes were opened to the plot, but it was too late to do anything about it. The law he had signed into effect was the law of the Medes and Persians. It was irrevocable. So Daniel, the great man of God who had served Babylon and then Persia with such exceptional distinction, was thrown into the lions' den as the king himself uttered a type of prayer: "May your God, whom you serve continually, rescue you!" (6:17). The king himself seemed to "catch" Daniel's bold, confident faith—because faith is contagious, isn't it?

CONFIDENT FAITH IS CONTAGIOUS

Darius tossed and turned all night. He could not eat and he could not sleep. Early the next morning, Darius ran to the lions' den, calling out, "'Daniel, servant of the living God, has your God, whom you serve continually, been able to rescue you from the lions?' Daniel answered, 'O king, live forever! My God sent his angel, and he shut the mouths of the lions. They have not hurt me'" (6:20–22). The overjoyed Darius scooped Daniel up out of the den, then immediately executed the men who had hatched the plot. He then proceeded to issue a decree that everyone in his kingdom was to fear and reverence the God of Daniel. Listen to Darius' testimony: "For he is the living God and he endures forever; his kingdom will not be destroyed, his dominion will never end" (6:26). God was glorified!

Which makes me wonder what my choices really reveal. When I pray, *God, be glorified in my life,* do I truly mean it? Am I willing to back up that request with choice after choice after choice to lay everything on the line . . .

reputation, position, education . . .

ministry, marriage, motives . . .

safety, success, strategy . . .

family, future, finances . . .

children, career, comfort . . .

dreams, desires, duties . . .

time, talents, treasures . . .

My whole life

. . . and trust it *all* to Him?

If you and I rarely exercise our faith, how can we be surprised when it's too weak for anyone to notice? Too weak to move others to recognize and acknowledge that our God is God? Too weak to be contagious? Daniel's choice to trust God repeatedly, regardless of how difficult or dangerous the situation was, impresses me that he wanted to serve a God who is God. If God was unable to come through for him—if He was unable to "push the wheelbarrow across the tightrope over Niagara Falls"—then He wasn't a God worth knowing. Or serving. Or risking his life for.

But the truth was that Daniel's God is God. With years of experience to back him up, he knew when he prayed that he was speaking to a living Person who would listen and respond to him. Again and again, as he had relied on God, God had been there for him. God had intervened miraculously in his circumstances and honored his trust in many ways.

But even more than the knowledge that God is real, Daniel was supremely confident that the living God of the universe was committed to him. He had established a personal, covenant relationship with the God of Abraham, Isaac, and Jacob. This confidence comes through clearly when he relates, "I prayed to the LORD *my* God . . ." (9:4, emphasis mine). Daniel knew that God was his, and he was God's. And it was this covenant relationship with God that is the bedrock of the Daniel Prayer. There was not a shred of doubt in Daniel's mind that God would hear his prayer. And God would answer.

CONFIDENT FAITH IN GOD'S COVENANT

Daniel would have entered into a covenant with God as a result of growing up a Jewish boy. The covenant was claimed by his parents, who would have had him circumcised on the eighth day of his life as an outward sign of it. Daniel's willing participation in the sacrificial system and the ceremonies in the temple further solidified his relationship with God.

Even in his old age, his memories of the temple sacrifices were precious to him because his participation had been heartfelt, not just ritualistic or traditional (9:21). He knew the living God was his God. When God had come through for him when he had made his choices again and again to trust Him completely under great pressure and risk to himself, he was increasingly confident that God claimed him also.

A covenant relationship with God is a vitally important necessity in prayer. While God can hear and answer any prayer He chooses, when you and I come to Him in a covenant relationship, we are guaranteed He will listen to us and will answer us. So, before beginning the actual words of the Daniel Prayer, it's to our benefit to determine if we are in a covenant relationship with God. Are you? I am.

I know that I am in a covenant relationship with God. My confidence is based on the first choice I described to you. The one I made when I was eight or nine years of age when I confessed my sin, asked God to forgive me, and placed my trust in Jesus as my Savior and Lord. Although with my child's mind I didn't understand the full scope of my choice at the time, looking back I know that's when I entered into a covenant relationship with God.

On the night Jesus was betrayed, He instituted an ordinance with His disciples that we keep today and refer to as Holy Communion. After the dinner, which was His last supper before His death on the Cross, He took an ordinary loaf of bread, broke it, and gave each of His disciples a piece as He explained it represented His body that would be broken for them. In the same manner, He took the cup of wine on the table, gave them each a sip, and expanded His explanation slightly when He said it represented His blood of the new covenant that would be poured out for the forgiveness of their sin.[4]

A covenant is a legal agreement between two or more parties, as in a treaty or formal agreement between nations. Or a land covenant between the buyer and the seller of property. Or a marriage covenant between husband and wife. The old biblical covenant with God is the one Daniel entered into through the Jewish laws, ceremonies, and sacrifices.

The new covenant I entered into is one that Jesus established by fulfilling the old covenant perfectly through His life and death. I entered into the new covenant as I "drank the cup" of His blood when I claimed His sacrifice on the Cross to make atonement for my sin. And as I "ate the bread" of His body when I took Him into my heart and gave Him access to every part of my life. The incredible, glorious truth is that once I entered into a covenant relationship with Him, He entered into that relationship with me, and I am His. Forever.

God's covenant, and all the privileges that it offers, became exceedingly meaningful to me the day after our house was robbed. Everything of real value was taken from me. All my silver, including the knife I had used to cut our wedding cake, jewelry that had marked milestones since childhood, my husband's wedding band, furniture, a camera with pictures of my children, everything my beloved grandmother had left me . . . gone.

The shattered frame of the front door seemed to hold echoes of the violence that thieves had used as they forced their way into our home. That night, having been warned by the police that the robbers would likely strike again, I was almost frozen with the shock of fear. I realized I was not safe, nor was anything or anyone in my house. I lay stiffly in bed—the same bed that I had found with the covers neatly folded back, and the cases removed from the pillows as the thieves used them as sacks to carry off my things. I was wide-eyed and terrified!

That night, I was finally able to get to sleep by focusing not on the things that had been taken, but on the things that I could never lose. I focused on the believer's birthright, given to those who enter into a covenant relationship with God, that guarantees . . .

Acceptance by God, with access to Him 24/7,

Blessing upon blessing upon blessing because I am His beloved,

Confidence that I've been chosen by Him,

Deliverance from the penalty and the power of sin,

Enlightenment to understand spiritual things, and
    eternal life that will never end,

Forgiveness of all my sin—past, present, and future,
Grace for every situation and need,

Hope for my tomorrows, and
    a Heavenly Home being prepared for me,

An inheritance that is kept for me in Heaven,

Justification so that in God's sight I am right with Him,

Knowledge of truth . . .

His love that will never let me go,
    His life that is abundant, full, and free,

His mercy that gives me less than I deserve,

His nearness regardless of where I am or what I'm doing,
Oneness with Him,

His power that's unlimited and
    His peace that passes all understanding,

His quickening into new life within,

Redemption from a meaningless, empty, superficial
    existence,

The divine seal of His Spirit placed within me,
    . . . and the list keeps going on and on.[5]

A covenant relationship with God is the equivalent of a legal promise to which He binds Himself so that you and I can take Him at His word with absolute confidence. It's His guarantee—*signed with His own blood.*

When have you entered into that covenant? Don't assume that you have. Don't hope that you have. Don't think that you have. You must *know* you have if you are going to effectively pray in such a way that Heaven is moved and nations are changed. If you are not sure . . . if there is any doubt whatsoever that you are in a covenant relationship with God, make sure. Right now. Pray a prayer something like this:

Dear Lord God of Daniel and Father of Jesus Christ,

I worship You as a covenant keeping God. Your word is as good as Your bond. Thank You for inviting me to enter into a covenant with You. I earnestly desire to be assured that You are committed to me forever. I long to belong to You. So right now, I confess to You that I am a sinner and have no merit of my own to deserve or earn this privilege. Instead, I have a strong tendency to do the wrong thing. To sin. So I confess to you my _____ *(fill in the blank with specific sins that come to your mind). I'm willing to turn away from my sin. To stop sinning, but I need Your help.*

I believe Jesus died on the Cross for me. Right now I choose to "drink the cup" of His blood shed on the Cross, applying His death to make atonement for my sin. Please forgive me and cleanse me of all my sin and guilt. And I choose to "eat the bread" of His body, surrendering every part of my life to His authority. Please come into my heart and be Lord of my life. I believe Jesus rose up from the dead to give to me eternal life.

I understand that eternal life means that Heaven is now my home, but I also understand that it includes the

believer's birthright that floods me with blessing after
blessing. Without doubt, the most precious blessing
of all is entering into this covenant and a personal love
relationship with You. Thank You for hearing this prayer. I
take You at Your word. I climb into the wheelbarrow and
trust myself to You completely. Forever. Amen.[6]

Signed: _____

Date: _____

Praise God! You have entered into a permanent covenant with the living God! You are eternally secured! The covenant does not depend on your ability to "keep" it, but on His ability to keep you. And Jesus made it clear that no one visible or invisible . . . not even yourself . . . *no one* can ever take you from your Father's hand.[7] Now that you are confident of your covenant relationship with God, you too can pray to the Lord *your* God, knowing that He will hear your prayer and answer you. What an awesome privilege!

Daniel was not only confident in his covenant relationship with God, but he was confident in God's character. He knew who the Person was to whom he was speaking.

CONFIDENT FAITH IN GOD'S CHARACTER

The Daniel Prayer begins dramatically with a declaration of praise for who God is. It begins with worship as Daniel focuses his faith on the Center-Point. It addresses God with awe and wonder as well as tenderness and intimacy. It reminds us that when we pray, we are actually communicating with a living Person who has . . .

> eyes to see us,
>
> ears to hear us,
>
> feet that swiftly come to our aid,
>
> hands to hold us,
>
> a mind that thinks on us,
>
> and a heart to love us.

As I listen to prayers prayed publicly in large gatherings and corporately in smaller settings, it amazes me to hear people immediately plunge into telling God "stuff." They go into detail about their own needs or someone's circumstances as though God needs to be informed. They can begin expressing a passionate desire for spiritual things like revival or their longing to see people respond to the Gospel. All of which may be valid. But to plunge into those things first? Without taking a moment to focus on the One to whom they are speaking?

I shared with you in the previous chapter the difference that it makes in my perspective and in my spirit when I make the time to center down on who God is. And I do this at the beginning of my prayer, before I pour out my list of complaints or problems or needs or worries or fears. Because my problems don't loom as large when contrasted with who God is. My future doesn't look so hopeless. My fears don't seem so legitimate. My worries don't seem so real. Focusing on the character of the One to whom I am speaking calms my spirit, lifts my eyes, and encourages my faith as I begin to pray.

And faith is a necessity if our prayers are going to move Heaven and change nations. The Bible says that when we come to God in prayer, we must believe that He is who He says He is, and that He will answer our prayer when we earnestly seek Him.[8] So it's no surprise that the Daniel Prayer begins with worship of the living God.

WORSHIP GOD FOR HIS FAITHFULNESS

As Daniel began to pray, at the forefront of his mind were the experiences he had had over his eighty-plus years of the faithfulness of God to him. God had not protected him from bad things. God had allowed Daniel to be kidnapped, enslaved, emasculated, endangered, threatened, betrayed, accused, and fed to lions! BUT God had never forsaken him. God had been with him every moment of every day. Daniel would never forget . . .

God's faithfulness to give him favor with the chief of the eunuchs and with his guard when he had come to Babylon, so that Daniel's request for food that had not first been sacrificed to Babylonian gods was honored.

God's faithfulness to make his three friends and himself healthier and smarter on a vegetarian diet than all the other Jewish young men who ate the rich food of the king's court that also gave tribute to the pagan gods.

God's faithfulness to enable his three friends and himself to pass their final exams with flying colors so that they were evaluated by the king to be the best of the best.

God's faithfulness to cause the chief of the king's guard to pause in his determination to carry out the order of execution, giving Daniel an opportunity to request a delay from the king.

God's faithfulness to move the king to grant the request.

God's faithfulness to put Daniel to sleep, then give him the very same dream the king had, along with its meaning.

God's faithfulness to give him clarity of thought and word as he related the dreams and their interpretation to the king, boldly refusing any personal credit and instead, giving all the glory to God.

God's faithfulness to spare his life and that of the other wise men when the king acknowledged the accuracy of the telling of his dreams and their interpretation.

God's faithfulness to give him the courage and boldness to read the handwriting on the wall, pronouncing judgment on Belshazzar, Nebuchadnezzar's successor, in the midst of the drunken king's orgy.

And when he had consistently maintained his center on God in prayer despite the death threat, God had not prevented him from the trauma of being thrown into the lions' den, but He had been faithful to shut the mouths of the lions, and thus deliver him.

It's no wonder that Daniel began his prayer with worship of God for His faithfulness: "O Lord, the great and awesome God, who keeps his covenant of love with all who love him and obey his commands" (9:4). He knew by experience that God keeps His covenant.

What experiences have you had of God's faithfulness? Have you been so focused on the tragedies or the troubles, the struggles or the setbacks, the poor health or the broken home, the divorce or the disease, that you have lost sight of God's faithfulness to be right there with you, then bring you through? Take a few moments and reflect on your life. Make a list of the times when you have glimpsed God's faithfulness to you, then praise Him.

Jeremiah, whose book Daniel had been reading when he was prompted to pray, bore witness himself to hard times. He himself had preached for over sixty years, warning his people of God's imminent judgment if they did not repent. As far as we know, he never received even one positive response to his message. And in the end, he lived to see his prophecies fulfilled when Nebuchadnezzar destroyed Jerusalem. Jeremiah wrote a very moving testimony: "I remember my affliction and my wandering, the bitterness and the gall. I well remember them, and my soul is downcast within me. Yet this I call to mind and therefore I have hope. Because of the LORD's great love we are not consumed, for his compassions never fail. They are new every morning; great is your faithfulness."[9]

WORSHIP GOD FOR HIS RIGHTEOUSNESS

God's judgment that Jeremiah kept warning about and people kept saying would not come, came. While Daniel had been swept up in the first deportation, there were two more. In the third one, Nebuchadnezzar leveled Jerusalem. The nation was decimated. The people were captured and enslaved. It was horrific!

As Daniel reflected on what he now knew sixty-seven years later—that all the dire warnings of impending judgment that Jeremiah and other prophets had issued had been fulfilled to even the smallest detail—he was confident that God had done the right thing. However, instead of expressing bitterness, anger, resentment, or offense with God for allowing evil to have the upper hand, Daniel prayed, "Lord, you are righteous" (9:7).

Not only was Daniel acknowledging the "rightness" of God's dealings with his nation and the world, but he was acknowledging God's rightness in the way He had dealt with Daniel. Think about it. Daniel's suffering. His separation from family and loved ones. His slavery. The stripping of his identity. His success that constantly seemed to be challenged. His absolute confidence in the righteousness of God seems amazing in light of what God had allowed him to go through.

Which makes me wonder. Could you and I honestly say the same thing? What about

if you were fired from your job . . .

if your spouse walked out . . .

if you were diagnosed with a deadly disease . . .

if your reputation was destroyed . . .

if your retirement evaporated . . .

if your house burned to the ground . . .

if a car accident left you paralyzed . . .

if you went through what Daniel went through, would you be tempted as Job was, to "curse God and die"?[10]

Or, would you pray as Daniel prayed, *Lord, You are righteous*? How could Daniel say that, much less think that?

What about . . .

if terrorists unload a dirty bomb on Manhattan . . .

if California falls into the Pacific when a massive earthquake erupts along the San Andreas fault . . .

if the economy collapses so that it takes a month's wage to buy a loaf of bread . . .

if it doesn't rain on our farmlands for three years . . .

if Ebola suddenly breaks out all over America . . .

would you be tempted to cry out, *God, where are You? This is so wrong . . .*

How can you and I truly believe that God does the right thing when really wrong things happen to us, to our loved ones, to our nation, and to our world? We can confidently say God does the right thing because God is righteous. That's His character. He never does the wrong thing. He cannot be anything other than Himself.

And He is righteous. All the time.

Our own ideas of what is right and wrong are just a small reflection of His. What a difference it would make in our perspective if we didn't look at God through the lens of our circumstances, but looked instead at our circumstances through the lens of who God is.

WORSHIP GOD FOR HIS GOODNESS

In many ways, this struggle to see things the way God sees them goes back to the Garden of Eden. In the very beginning of human history, Satan tempted the first woman, Eve, to doubt the goodness of God. She lived in Paradise, literally, and was the adored wife of the first man, Adam. She could have had anything she wanted. Except for one thing. She had been forbidden to eat the fruit from the tree of the knowledge of good and evil. The restriction was God's test of the first couple's love and devotion to Him.

The test was intensified when Satan slithered up and suggested to Eve, "God knows that when you eat of it your eyes will be opened, and you will be like God, knowing good and evil."[11] In other words, *Eve, God knows this fruit is really good. But He's mean and doesn't want you to enjoy life to the fullest. Besides, He's also jealous and keeps all the best stuff to Himself.*

Eve failed the test miserably. She bought into the argument that God was holding out on her. That He really isn't a good God. So she took the forbidden fruit, ate it, then shared it with Adam who ate it also in blatant disobedience of what God had said. As a result, her eyes were opened, but in a way God never intended. She knew good, but she now knew she was separated from it. And she knew evil, because she now knew also she was saturated in it.

As a result, sin and death came into the human race. And into Eve's own family. She lived to witness her firstborn son, Cain, murder her second-born son, Abel. I can only imagine how many moments of how many days of how many years of the rest of her life Eve struggled with, "If only . . ." "If only I had obeyed God's word." "If only I had trusted God's goodness." "If only I had had confidence in God's character . . ." "If only . . ."

What bad thing, or unjust thing, or abusive thing, or tragic thing, or hurtful thing, or evil thing has happened to you? Something that was unexpected, unwanted, and unplanned. Just plain wrong. And in the midst of the emotional wreckage, did Satan slither up beside you and hiss into your ear, *God is mean. He can't be trusted. He could have prevented this. He's out to get you. Do you remember the sin you committed back when . . . ? Well, He remembers. This is payback. Because God is not good.*

While those may not have been Satan's exact words, did he use words that were similar? Has he caused you to doubt the goodness of God?

If you have the slightest suspicion that God is holding out on you . . .

If you have the slightest doubt that He wants what's best for you . . .

If you have even the slightest doubt that God is truly good . . .

you will struggle praying the Daniel Prayer. You will lack confidence in the character of the One to whom you are praying. And that will make a huge impact on the prayer's effectiveness.

So . . . take a moment now to pinpoint your doubt of God's goodness and what your reasons are for having it. Tell Him why you are afraid to "get into the wheelbarrow" and trust Him completely. Ask Him to give you experiences, as He did Daniel, that will help to build your confidence in Him. Then open your eyes to look past the experiences to the God who is in the shadows behind them.

While Daniel could have had many reasons to doubt the goodness of God because of the things that God had allowed to happen to him, he did not. He had eyes to see past the circumstances into the very nature of God. He knew that even though bad things had happened, God was merciful, forgiving, and good.

Toward the end of Daniel's life, one of his memories that stood out was what had happened to his three friends, Meshach, Shadrach, and Abednego, shortly after they had been elevated to provincial governors. It was an experience that revealed that God may allow extremely bad things to happen to His children, not because He is not good, but because He has a greater purpose in mind.

Daniel recalled that the king had issued a proclamation that all of his officials throughout Babylon were to come to the Plain of Shinar. Since Daniel had been assigned to the royal court, he had been exempt from the obligation to respond to the king's edict. But his three friends were required to attend the official dedication of a gold-plated replica of Nebuchadnezzar that was ninety feet tall. While it was just a wooden pole overlaid with gold, on the flat plain it must have looked like the New World Trade Center in Lower Manhattan.

When all the Babylonian officials gathered, they were informed that when they heard the band strike up, they were to fall down and worship the image of gold. If they did not, they would be thrown into a furnace of fire. It's almost eerie to realize that Daniel's three friends were faced with a choice that God's children are currently being faced with on that same plain and its surrounding areas today. In effect, they were to renounce their religion and their God, and pledge their allegiance to their captor's god, or face a gruesome, cruel death.

Today, the demand on some Christians is to convert to Islam or be tortured, beheaded, crucified, shot, raped, or burned alive. Thousands in the world today have followed the splendid example of Meshach, Shadrach, and Abednego. When they were told to either bow down to the golden image or refuse and be burned alive, they did not even bend slightly. As soon as the sound of the music began, everyone as far as the eye could see fell prostrate. When the movement of the people grew still, and the strains of the music wafted through the dusty air, it was apparent that everyone had complied. Everyone . . . except for three young Hebrew men who remained ramrod straight.

Immediately someone informed the king of their insubordination. They were arrested and taken before Nebuchadnezzar, who was "furious with rage." He told them he would give them one more chance to bow down. If they did not, they would be burned alive because "what god will be able to rescue you from my hand?" (3:16).

Their response was an expression of classic, centered, confident faith: "O Nebuchadnezzar, we do not need to defend ourselves before you in this matter. If we are thrown into the blazing furnace, the God we serve is able to save us from it, and he will rescue us from your hand, O king. But even if he does not, we want you to know, O king, that we will not serve your gods or worship the image of gold you have set up" (3:16–18). They had "stepped into the wheelbarrow" as they flung themselves on the mercy of their God, trusting Him completely!

The king was enraged. Although he had recognized them earlier as three of the best and brightest of his captives, and although he had placed them in prominent positions of leadership, the Bible records his attitude toward the three young men changed. He ordered the furnace heated seven times hotter than usual, commanded his strongest soldiers to tie them up fully clothed with robes, trousers, and turbans, then had the three young men thrown into the fire. The flames were so intense that they incinerated the men who threw Meshach, Shadrach, and Abednego into the furnace. Expecting to see the young men also quickly burned to a crisp, Nebuchadnezzar instead jumped up out of his seat and demanded of his guards, "Weren't there three men that we tied up and threw into the fire? . . . Look! I see four men walking around in the fire, unbound and unharmed, and the fourth looks like a son of the gods" (3:24–25). God Himself had shown up! He walked in the midst of the fire with His children.

This is a lesson for you and me to wrap our confidence around. When God allows us to experience a fiery furnace, He promises to experience it with us.[12] Because He is good!

With a dramatically different tone to his voice, the king respectfully asked the young men to step out of the furnace. When they did, everyone gathered around to touch, to look, to sniff, and to thoroughly examine them, but they found that not even one hair of their heads was singed. Their robes had no smell of fire or smoke. Even Nebuchadnezzar knew he had witnessed a miraculous intervention of the one true living God. Which was how he responded, "Praise be to the God of Shadrach, Meshach, and Abednego, who has sent his angel and rescued his servants!" (3:28).

Once again, God was glorified and His servants were honored with promotions in their positions of service.

Shortly thereafter, the king himself related the most remarkable story. His story. He was wealthy, powerful, lacking in nothing, on top of the world. Although God had warned him of the dangers of pride and arrogance, Nebuchadnezzar did not heed the warning. One year later he "was walking on the roof of the royal palace of Babylon" when he bragged, "Is not this the great Babylon I have built as the royal residence, by my mighty power and for the glory of my majesty?" (4:28–30). Immediately he came under God's judgment and literally went insane. For seven years he lived like an animal. At the end of that time, he raised his eyes toward Heaven in what must have been a silent, humble plea for mercy and forgiveness, and God heard his prayer! His sanity was restored, as was his kingdom and his throne and his power so that he was even greater than before.

Listen to his testimony in his own words: "Now I, Nebuchadnezzar, praise and exalt and glorify the King of heaven, because everything he does is right and all his ways are just. And those who walk in pride he is able to humble" (4:37). That's God's amazing grace!

I wonder if Nebuchadnezzar's story was on Daniel's mind when he recalled confidently, "The Lord our God is merciful and forgiving" (9:9). Because God is good.

Manasseh was one of the kings of Judah who learned by hard personal experience that God is good. He was more evil than the surrounding pagan kings and deliberately led God's people away from God. So he came under radical, severe judgment. Bound in bronze shackles with a hook in his nose, he was captured, dragged to Assyria, and imprisoned by the king who was the ISIS commander of his day.

In the extremity of his distress, Manasseh humbled himself and cried out when in prison to the Lord, who heard his prayer, set him free, returned him to Jerusalem, and restored him to the throne.[13] Because, "The Lord our God is merciful and forgiving." That's God's amazing grace!

Saul of Tarsus was a self-righteous Pharisee whose mission in life was to purge the world of followers of Jesus Christ. He adopted a scorched-earth policy, going door to door to seize Christians, throw them into prisons, and put them to death. He took his mission outside of Jerusalem with the intention of chasing them down all the way to Syria. But on the Damascus road he was suddenly confronted by the risen, living Lord Jesus Himself, who asked him why he was persecuting Him.

Saul was not only flattened, but physically blinded by the encounter and had to be led into Damascus by his associates. Once there, God's purpose for his life was explained, and he responded by committing his life to the One he had formerly been persecuting. Not only was Saul's name changed to Paul,[14] but his entire life was radically changed. He became a proclaimer of the Gospel he had fought to destroy and the author of much of the New Testament. Because, "The Lord our God is merciful and forgiving." That's God's amazing grace!

What's your story? How has God demonstrated His goodness and amazing grace in your life? What have you done or said that makes you think you are beyond God's grace? If God could forgive and change a Nebuchadnezzar . . . if He could forgive and change a Manasseh . . . if He could forgive and change a Saul into a Paul . . . why do you think He can't do the same for you? The key is that you must turn to Him.

Daniel held tightly to the key as he turned to God in prayer. Because he was confident in God's mercy, forgiveness, and goodness, he was confident there was hope for his people. He believed there was hope for them even though they were being held captive in Babylon, because he knew there had been hope for them years before when they were being held captive in Egypt.

WORSHIP GOD FOR HIS GREATNESS

As Daniel continued to pray, he expressed his supreme confidence in the greatness of God as he reflected on His power: "Now, O Lord our God, who brought your people out of Egypt with a mighty hand . . ." You've . . . "made for yourself a name that endures to this day" (9:15).

God's name is synonymous with greatness. And other than Creation and the resurrection of Jesus Christ, there has never been a greater demonstration of God's power than when He delivered His people from slavery in Egypt.[15]

God's people, Abraham's descendants, had migrated to Egypt as a result of severe famine in Canaan. They lived comfortably in Egypt for approximately 350 years, multiplying into a small nation. Their numbers alarmed Pharaoh, who proceeded to contain them by enslaving them, which he did for 70 years. Under cruel bondage, they cried out to God to send a deliverer.

He sent Moses, a man who had been born to Hebrew parents but, in a miraculous turn of events, had been raised in the king's palace by the daughter of Pharaoh. As a young man, his ties with Pharaoh had been severed and he had been exiled from Egypt. For forty years he lived on the backside of the desert, herding sheep and living a relatively quiet, nondescript existence.

But then God showed up. He dramatically confronted Moses through a burning bush in the desert. He commanded Moses to return to Egypt and demand that Pharaoh let His people go. After some argument, Moses reluctantly obeyed. Understandably, when Pharaoh hardened his heart and refused to comply, things got worse. With a small spark of hope having been kindled with Moses' appearance, then quickly squelched by Pharaoh's cruel order that their oppression be increased, God's people had become even more hopeless and discouraged.

God stepped in and took charge. He sent a series of ten plagues to Egypt as His judgment for Pharaoh's refusal to let His people go. After each plague, Pharaoh was given the opportunity to repent and let God's people go. Although Pharaoh said he would obey, he then changed his mind, hardened his heart, and refused. So the plagues just kept coming, one after another.

First, God turned the Nile to blood, then frogs covered the land. Gnats swarmed, followed by flies. The livestock were killed, then the animals and people broke out in painful boils. Hail fell from the sky, and locusts covered the land, destroying everything the hail had left. Darkness descended before the last and most terrible of all the plagues: the death of all the firstborn, both men and animals.

In the end, of course, Pharaoh relented and let God's people go. It's estimated that approximately two million Hebrew men, women, and children walked out of Egypt, led by Moses.

But the plagues were not the greatest demonstration of God's power. Once Moses led God's people out, Pharaoh changed his mind and began to pursue what he surely saw as his disappearing labor force and the resulting collapse of the Egyptian economy.

To their horror, the newly freed slaves looked behind them and saw an approaching dust cloud that indicated Pharaoh and his army were just over the horizon. They had no escape route. On one side were mountains, on the other side was the desert, and in front of them was the Red Sea. They were trapped! In their terror, they turned on Moses, accusing him of having led them out of Egypt only to die in the wilderness. But like Daniel, Moses was confident in God's great power. He instructed them, "Do not be afraid. Stand firm and you will see the deliverance of the LORD."[16]

What the Israelites saw was a thick cloud that formed between Pharaoh's army and themselves, so that they were protected. Darkness fell, further blinding the enemy. Then all night, a strong wind rose up that parted the waters of the sea, so that in the morning there was a pathway of dry ground through it. Dry ground. Not a muddy mess. The waters formed liquid walls on their right and on their left as the Israelites quickly went through the sea to the other side.

When the last Israelite had made it to safety, the cloud lifted. Pharaoh's army saw that they were escaping and so recklessly pursued them on that same dry pathway through the sea. Except this time, at God's command, the sea walls collapsed on the pursuing enemy. The water returned to its former level with no markers to indicate the Red Sea had become a watery grave for hundreds of Egyptian troops, horses, and chariots. "When the Israelites saw the great power the LORD displayed against the Egyptians, the people feared the LORD and put their trust in him . . ."[17] They burst into a song of praise known as the Song of Moses that undoubtedly Daniel knew by heart.[18] It's a song that is repeated throughout the Old Testament. It's a song that exults in the greatness of God's majesty and power.

As Daniel recalled this supreme, historic demonstration of God's unparalleled power to set His people free, he was compelled to plead with God, *Do it again!* If God had been moved to action as a result of the cries of the Israelites in Egypt, surely the same God would be moved to action as a result of the cries of the Israelites in Babylon. And if God could change Pharaoh's heart long enough so that God's people were set free, then the same God could change the Persian emperor's heart so that the Israelites were set free once again. *Couldn't He?*

And if God heard the cries of His people in Egypt and in Persia so that Heaven was moved to answer, why would He not hear our prayers today for our nation? For the revival of the church? For our families? And if God changed the heart of Pharaoh in Egypt, and the kings in Babylon and Persia, why cannot the very same God change the hearts of our political and religious leaders, and the hearts of others today? If God could change the nations of Babylon, Persia, and Israel, why can't He change our nation?

He can, can't He?

PLEADING WITH CONFESSION

We called my grandfather on my father's side Daddy Graham. He was a tall, soft-spoken, true Southern gentleman. He wore black-and-white spectator shoes and a broad-brimmed hat pulled down on his brow, but only when he was going to church or to the nearby S&W Cafeteria. For most of the week, he dressed in faded, well-worn work clothes that carried with them the "sweet essence of agriculture" because he was a dairy farmer.

I was raised hearing from my father how Daddy Graham made him get up at 3:00 a.m. every morning to milk about fourteen cows before he went to school. Daddy didn't have an alarm to wake him up. What he had was the warning from Daddy Graham that if he overslept he would get a bucket of cold water in his face. Which he did. Once. From then on Daddy was up on time.

Daddy Graham also grew the corn that he used to feed his cows. The hottest I've ever been was when I walked through the cornfield that was next to my grandparents' house one summer afternoon. I can verify that in the heart of a cornfield, there is no breeze at all. Just stifling heat. When I emerged from the field, I was dripping wet and covered with what felt like tiny paper cuts that the stiff leaves of the corn stalks had left on my arms. That was in the summer time.

But after the corn was harvested, the bare ground of that cornfield hardened. Within a fairly short period of time, weeds and grass would begin to take over. Before Daddy Graham could plant the next crop of corn the following spring, he had to plow up the fallow earth and remove the weeds, so that it would be soft enough to receive the seeds of corn that he would then plant, and absorb the rain and sunshine that he hoped would follow.

The nation of Judah had once been a fertile field that had grown "crops" of righteousness—people who loved, obeyed, and served the Lord. But as a result of her sin, God had raised up the Babylonians as His instruments of judgment. As we have already considered, the consequences were that Daniel and his people were removed and taken eight hundred miles east, where they were enslaved in a foreign land. In essence, the land and the people had lain "fallow," unplowed for sixty-seven years.

So the Daniel Prayer was a plea for God . . .

To plow up the fallow ground.

To forgive his people their sins.

To release his people from judgment.

To "heal the land" and bring life back to Jerusalem.

To put God back at the center of their national life

by reviving authentic worship and restoring the temple.

Bottom line, the Daniel Prayer was a plea for God to be glorified once again through their personal and national lives. It was a prayer for national restoration and revival.

If that sounds familiar, it's because again and again over the last few years we have heard God's promise to King Solomon in

2 Chronicles 7:14 invoked on behalf of our nation: "If my people, who are called by my name, will humble themselves and pray and seek my face and turn from their wicked ways, then will I hear from heaven and will forgive their sin and will heal their land." I have used it. I have prayed it. I have claimed it. I have built messages around it. It was a foundational verse for a prayer that I wrote that was prayed in over 44,000 services for our nation in 2014.[1]

So . . . instead of experiencing revival, why does our nation seem to be collapsing until we are morally and spiritually bankrupt? Why are we witnessing a hell-bent charge into the miry pits of sin and secularism? Why, instead of being healed, have we seemed to become more polarized than ever? I wonder . . . Have we been missing something? Overlooking . . . neglecting . . . ignoring something? Maybe . . .

Out of the sixteen verses covered by Daniel's prayer in chapter nine, twelve of them confess sin. Not "their" sin, but "our" sin. All through his prayer, Daniel uses plural pronouns. Which reveals to me that he was as aware of sin in his own heart as he was in the hearts of his people. Could that be what's missing? I wonder.

We may never have another Great Awakening in our nation until you and I stop pointing our finger at "them" and deal with the sin in our own hearts and lives. An old-timey revivalist, Gypsy Smith, was asked where revival begins. He answered, *I draw a circle around myself and make sure everything in that circle is right with God.* Which prompts the question, if we have yet to see revival fire fall in our nation, could the problem be within the circle? Could the problem be with you and me?

CONFESSION OF PERSONAL SIN

Before leading a seminar several years ago, I set aside ten days to work on the seven different messages that I would be giving. On the first day, I pulled out my Bible, my pencil, and my legal pad, said a quick prayer asking for God's blessing, then began to work through the passage of Scripture that would be the basis for the first message. As I sought to break open the passage, I got nothing. No real revelation or understanding at all. I knew I was just spinning my mental and spiritual wheels, so I concluded that my weariness was dulling my mind. I decided to put myself to bed with the intention of beginning in the morning when I felt more alert and fresh.

The next morning, after a good night's sleep, a brisk walk and a substantial breakfast, I felt refreshed. So I sat down at my desk where my Bible was still open from the night before, picked up my pen, and held it poised over the legal pad to begin writing my first thoughts. Once again I prayed, this time with more expectancy. I then proceeded to read and reread the passage of Scripture. Nothing. I prayed again, except this time there was an insistent edge to my prayer as I explained to the Lord I only had a limited time to prepare the messages, I had hundreds of people who had paid to hear them who would be arriving now within nine days, and I needed His help. Nothing.

And then, there seemed to be a small whisper in my heart. *Anne, I don't want to talk about the messages. I want to talk about you.* Recognizing the still, small voice of the Spirit, I replied honestly, *I don't want to talk about me. There's no time. I want to talk about these messages. After I have prepared and delivered them, then we will talk about me.* Nothing. Only now there was dead silence that was becoming quite loud. With a panicked pace to my heart, I pondered what was going on. I knew there was no way I could prepare the messages without His help, so the only option I could come up with was to talk about what He wanted to talk about. As quickly as I could.

So I got down on my knees, and I will confess there were tears on my face as I asked Him what He wanted to talk about. I was listening. Five days later He was still talking. About sin! In my life! Every time I opened my Bible a verse seemed to leap up off the page, indicting me for another sin I hadn't been aware of. It was awful. Painful. Humiliating. To the extreme.

This dialogue with a very holy God was triggered by a little book I was reading by another old-timey revivalist.[2] The third chapter was titled, "Preparing the Heart for Revival." He based his comments on Hosea 10:12, "Break up your unplowed ground; for it is time to seek the LORD, until he comes and showers righteousness on you."

The author explained that to experience revival, we must look to our own hearts and the spiritual ground that had perhaps become hardened over time. Like Daddy Graham and his cornfield, we must plow it up. We must examine the state of our own minds. We must reflect on our past actions. He cautioned that he did not mean that we were to glance at things, then make a general confession to God the way many of us do with, *Dear God, forgive me for all my many sins. Amen.* He challenged the reader to take pen and paper and write down each sin as it came to mind. Because our sins are committed one at a time, he said they must be reviewed and repented of one by one. To get the reader started, he included a list of sins that I have reworded slightly, but you will still get the point:

Ingratitude. List all the favors God has bestowed, before and after salvation. Which ones had I forgotten to thank Him for?

Losing Love for God. Consider how devastated I would be if my husband or children not only were lessened in their love for me, but increasingly loved someone or something else more. Was there evidence I was lessening in my love for Him?

Neglect of Bible Reading. Double-check to see if daily Bible reading had been pushed aside by an over-full schedule, or if, as I read my Bible, I was constantly preoccupied with other things. How long had it been since reading my Bible was a delight? Do I read it so casually that I don't even remember what it said when I finish?

Unbelief. Refusing to believe or to expect that He will give me what He has promised is to accuse Him of lying. What promise do I think He will not give me? What prayer do I think He will not answer?

Neglect of Prayer. I will put this one in my own words. Prayers are not spiritual chatter, offered without fervent, focused faith. Have I substituted wishing, daydreaming, or fantasizing for real prayer?

Lack of Concern for the Souls of Others. Standing by and watching friends, neighbors, coworkers, and even family members on their way to hell, yet not caring enough to warn them or pray for them or even admit that's where they will end up if they don't put their faith in Jesus. Have I become so politically correct that I don't apply the Gospel to those I know and love?

Neglect of Family. Putting myself and my needs before them. What effort am I making, what habit have I established, for my family's spiritual good when it requires personal sacrifice?

This list is painful, isn't it? But the revivalist wasn't finished. He kept going.

Love of the World and Material Things. Assess what I own. Do I think my possessions are mine? That my money is mine? That I can spend it or dispose of it as I choose?

Pride. Vanity about my appearance. More time spent in getting ready for church than preparing my heart and mind to worship when I get there. Am I offended, or even slightly irritated, if others don't notice my appearance?

Envy. Jealousy of those who seem more fruitful or gifted or recognizable than I am. Do I struggle with hearing others praised?

A Critical Spirit. God has given me a spirit of discernment. But do I use it to find fault with others who don't measure up to my standards?

Slander. Telling the truth with the intention of causing people to think less of a person. Whose faults, real or imagined, have I discussed behind their backs? Why have I?

Lack of Seriousness toward God. Showing disrespect for God by the way I sleep through my prayer time or show up late for church as though He doesn't really matter. Do I give Him the leftovers of my emotions, time, thoughts, money?

Lying. Designed deception. Anything that is contrary to the unvarnished truth. What have I said that was designed to impress someone, but it wasn't the whole truth? Or was an exaggeration of the truth?

Cheating. Treating others in a way I wouldn't want to be treated myself. Have I stopped short of treating others the way I would want to be treated?

Hypocrisy. Pretending to be something that I am not. Am I pretending to be anything I am not?

Robbing God. Wasting my time on things that have no eternal value. Exercising my God-given gifts and talents for a fee. What am I not doing for God that I am willing to do for others—for a price?

Temper. Losing patience with a child, coworker, friend, spouse, or staff member. What cross words have I spoken lately?

Bad Temper. Losing control of my emotions, thoughts, and words so that I abuse someone else verbally. Have I lost my temper?

Hindering Others. Taking someone else's time needlessly. Destroying someone's confidence because I hold them to an unreasonably high standard.

Arrogance. Accepting God's forgiveness while refusing to forgive myself or someone else.

That's quite a list! The original author gave instructions that after the reader had carefully considered each of the sins on the list, he or she was to go back and reread the list, writing down any other sins that come to mind. When that exercise was completed, he said to do it again. A third time.

CONFESSION OF PERSONAL SHAME

To humor this old man who is now in glory, I followed his instructions. The first time I went down the list, I finished with gratitude that not one of the sins described me! So with confidence and a little smugness, I read the list the second time. After this second reading I thought that if I stretched the meaning of some of the sins he listed, I could see the slight possibility of a few of them in my life.

Feeling very spiritual for being honest enough to glimpse traces of sin in my own heart, I read the list for the third time. And that's when I was laid bare. God used that list of sins to shine the light of His Truth deep down into the dark inner recesses of my heart where sin was lurking. It was like having a spiritual angiogram. The sins revealed went farther and broader than just those on the list. Altogether, my time of conviction, confession, and cleansing lasted for seven days!

God took seven days to clean me up. And I was in ministry! Seven days to point out sin I didn't even know I had. I had not been neglecting my daily Bible reading or prayer previously. I was deeply involved in studying, applying, and living out God's Word to the best of my ability. I was committed to sharing it with others. In fact, I had devoted most of my adult life to serving God outside of my home. How could I have allowed the sin to pile up like that in my heart and life? I was deeply ashamed. Humiliated before God. And still am.

In fact, I think one reason some of us, myself included, don't examine our hearts for sin is because we are so afraid we will find it. One thing I have discovered is that it takes courage to look deep within to see what God sees. It's painful to acknowledge that we're not as good, righteous, pure, or holy as we thought we were.

It's even more shameful to acknowledge that with my family background, and with all the time I spent in God's Word and in prayer, I should have known better. But like cobwebs in the corners of a dusty, unkempt attic room, my heart had held unconfessed sin. So for seven days I clung to the old rugged Cross. I discovered in a fresh, very personal way that the blood of Jesus is not just for unsaved sinners who come to the Cross for the first time, but for saved sinners who need to come back and back and back. Praise God! The blood of Jesus never runs out. It never loses its power to cleanse and to wash us as white as snow. *I know . . .*

Three days before my seminar was to begin, God indicated that He was finished convicting and cleansing. At least for that time. When I asked Him, *Are you sure? I don't want to miss anything.* He gave me a sweet, blessed assurance that I was cleansed of my sin and my shame, and filled with His Spirit. When I once again picked up my pad and pencil to work on the messages, my thoughts flowed freely. By the time the seminar began, I was prepared. While the people who attended had no idea what I had been through, I believe all of them sensed a freshness of power and renewed passion as I taught.

Looking back, I now know that what I had experienced was revival. Personal revival. It's what I have longed to see take place corporately so that the entire church is revived and our nation is restored. But one thing I have also learned is that genuine repentance of sin that is the key to revival is a gift from God. I could never have had the experience that I did if God Himself had not convicted me and led me through the steps of confession and cleansing. I could not have worked it up or faked it.

Which leads me back to the Daniel Prayer. I am convinced that the key to revival is repentance. And that the key to repentance is prayer. Not prayer that preaches at people. But prayer that is offered with wet eyes, a broken heart, and bent knees.

Daniel prayed with the words of a man who seemed to have a conscious awareness of his own sin as he prayed for the sin he saw in others. There was nothing judgmental or self-righteous in his words. I believe it's a lesson that must be learned if our prayers are going to move Heaven and change nations.

Just because our personal sins are not on public display or in national headlines does not mean we can ignore them. Sin is always sin. So . . . before we apply the Daniel Prayer to the sins of others, would you take a moment to search your own heart? Would you be courageous enough to read through the list of sins three times? Would you take a pencil and paper in hand to write down the sins that you see in yourself, and the sins not on the list that come to your mind? Then confess your sin. Tell God you are sorry. Ask Him to cleanse you. Of all of them.

Ask Him not to miss anything in your heart, mind, or life that needs the blood of Jesus. Do it now. Take as long as you need. Seven minutes, seven hours, seven days, seven weeks, seven months. Just do it. Plow up the fallow ground of your heart so He can send you showers of His blessing and righteousness. Draw a circle around yourself and make sure that everything in it is right with God . . . as He sees you. As we pray for revival, ask Him to let it begin with you.

Once our hearts are broken for our own sin, then we are ready to intercede with God for the sins of others.

CONFESSION OF NATIONAL SIN

Daniel began his prayer with worship of God for His faithfulness, as we have seen, but he then quickly confesses, "We have sinned and done wrong. We have been wicked and have rebelled; we have turned away from your commands and laws" (9:5). Like holding up a lantern to pierce the darkness, Daniel held up the light of who God is while he peered into his people's lives. Wrongdoing, wickedness, and willfulness became glaringly apparent.

According to Webster's dictionary, to do wrong is to live without a moral standard. To be wicked is to then substitute our own standard that we make up, which is morally bad and distorted. And the "standard" that is then substituted is promoted with a willfulness that is an obstinate, stubborn determination to do whatever we want.

Judah had been founded on faith in God and had had godly leaders in the past, but she had thrown away her time-honored moral standards. With no plumb line, she had plunged into idolatry and worse. And she had done so in willful disobedience to what she had known was right. As a result, she had come under God's judgment. Because while God is patient, He will not tolerate sin.

Is our nation where Judah was? We too seem to have thrown away our national moral standards, substituting what's right in our own eyes and doing so with a defiance that at times is breathtaking. Our city streets are filled with the sound of people marching to insist on their right to do what they please. Legislators pass laws that guarantee legal acceptance of sin. Movies and television programs glamorize sinful behavior and make it look enticingly pleasurable.

And it's all carried out with such determination that any voice raised in objection, or even raised in question, is silenced by ridicule and intimidation.

When did our nation's moral and spiritual foundation begin to crack so that it is now crumbling until it has almost disappeared? While there has never been a perfect golden age in our country's history, the disintegration of our national foundation of faith can be clearly seen in the statistics of life before 1962 and 1963 when prayer and Bible reading were removed from the public schools. Since 1963, academic achievement has dropped; teen pregnancy and juvenile crime have increased. Many public schools have metal detectors that the students have to pass through to enter the buildings. Law-enforcement officers patrol the halls, and the defiance of authority—any authority—makes classroom instruction almost impossible.[3] Separation of our church and state was never intended to be separation of state from God. But that's effectively what began to occur when God was forced out of our classrooms. This was a major intentional, national step on a path away from God that I believe has helped propel us to where we are today.

While we can certainly point to Supreme Court decisions in 1962 and 1963 that removed prayer and Bible reading from public schools as pivotal turning points in our nation's moral and spiritual downward spiral, I wonder if it began even earlier. Did it begin where Romans 1 indicates the early stage of God's wrath is initiated? And what is that early stage? It's when we abandon God by suppressing the truth—specifically the instinctive knowledge of God through Creation.[4]

You and I can walk outside and gaze on a clear, star-studded night sky, and unless you deliberately repress what your instincts are telling you, you will know there is Someone behind the design of the stars and planets and moon and sun and tides and seasons. When you experience a pregnancy or witness the birth of a baby, unless you deliberately repress your instincts, you know there is Someone behind the design of human life and the human body. To say that our universe and human life are some sort of cosmic accidents is like saying someone set off dynamite in a junkyard, and when the dust settled, a Rolex watch was the result. It doesn't make any logical, practical sense. And yet, that is purported to be the accepted view of the majority in our nation.

When God is rejected as Creator, it logically follows that we will not glorify Him nor be thankful to Him, because, after all, He really is irrelevant to life. If He even exists. So we glorify "science" and technology and man himself.

With all of the advanced education available today, we can legitimately claim to be smarter than any previous generation, yet we have become "fools" who have exchanged the glory of the Creator for created things.[5] We have exchanged the truth of Creation for the theory of evolution.

The theory of evolution, which teaches us that we came from nothing, we are going nowhere, that our lives have no purpose and meaning here other than to live for today, and that we are not accountable to anyone, has become broadly accepted as the explanation for the beginning of everything. Anyone running for high political office, including that of the presidency, is expected to answer a question about creationism versus evolution. If the person affirms his or her belief in Creation, the mocking laughter and ridicule becomes so loud it can dismantle and defeat even the most well-organized political machine.

We repress not only what we instinctively know about God in Creation, we repress what we instinctively know in our consciences. The Bible says we have a moral instinct stamped within us. We were born knowing right from wrong. But we repress this instinct again and again by the choices we make until we can no longer "hear" our conscience. We silence our moral alarm of guilt that tries to warn us we are doing the wrong thing through therapy. Or drugs. Or rationalizing that "everyone does it." Or even legitimizing wrong by legalizing it.

At this stage, having abandoned knowledge of the one, true, living God by rejecting Him as Creator and repressing our moral conscience, He begins to abandon us. He just backs away. Lifts His hand of blessing and lets us have our way that we keep insisting on having.

We think of God's judgment as fire and brimstone falling from Heaven as it did on Sodom and Gomorrah,[6] or the ground opening up and swallowing us,[7] or an invading army like the Babylonians sweeping in and destroying us, or some other dramatic divine disaster. And while those things can be signs of God's judgment, the worst judgment of all is for God to abandon us so that we are separated from Him. It's a judgment that is actually hell on earth.

If God is abandoning us as a nation, what is the evidence? It's worthwhile to trace the progression of sin and judgment that is described in Romans 1, and gives the first sign of evidence as increasing immorality: "Therefore God gave them over in the sinful desires of their hearts to sexual impurity for the degrading of their bodies with one another."[8]

The sexual revolution had been simmering for some time, rooted in a radical belief that all sexual morality is a form of oppression.[9] But the revolution came into full national view during the summer of 1967. It was enthusiastically promoted by people in Haight-Ashbury, San Francisco, who championed free sex, LSD, and rock 'n' roll. Two summers later, approximately 400,000 people gathered on a field in Woodstock, New York, to celebrate "free love." Fifty years later, the statistics reveal the high cost of free love: half of all first-time births are to unwed mothers; over 55 million unborn babies have been aborted; sexually transmitted diseases infect 110 million men and women each year; 39 million people have died of HIV/AIDS. Syndicated columnist Cal Thomas writes, "Sex sells but it also brings misery when misused."[10]

It's time to repent.

If we as a nation do not repent of our immorality, then we descend into the next stage of God's judgment and the evidence of His abandonment, which is homosexuality. Listen to His indictment: He "gave them over to shameful lusts. Even their women exchanged natural relations for unnatural ones. In the same way the men also abandoned natural relations with women and were inflamed with lust for one another. Men committed indecent acts with other men . . ."[11]

On June 26, 2015, in a five-to-four decision, the Supreme Court of the United States legalized same-sex marriage. In all fifty states.

Homosexuality has increasingly become accepted as a credible lifestyle. Because Americans are generous and goodhearted, we have embraced homosexuals because for the most part, the people we know living this lifestyle are nice people. Kind. Caring.

Smart. Fun. Interesting. Gifted. And so we rationalize, how could such wonderful people be so wrong and wicked and willful in God's eyes? Yet we don't search out what God thinks, because we have already abandoned Him for all practical purposes.

We have thought it was not "worthwhile to retain the knowledge of God," so "he gave them over to a depraved mind, to do what ought not to be done."[12] We no longer think straight. Pun intended. Our minds have twisted around the "evidence" that since homosexuals are born that way, then God intends for them to live in this lifestyle, approves of it, and blesses it. In fact, we are defiant in our willfulness, flaunting our right to sin as our president promotes the gay agenda worldwide by flying the LGBT flag next to the Stars and Stripes over the US embassies in Tel Aviv, London, Madrid, and other world capitals. Yet God does not approve or bless this lifestyle.

It's time to repent.

If we refuse to repent, we are abandoned further by God and we descend deeper into judgment. The next sign of God removing Himself from our national life is when we disintegrate morally and spiritually. And we are. Our nation is unraveling into a tangled maze of idiocy. Craziness. Children killing their parents, husbands killing their wives, husbands beating their wives, mothers killing their children, active shooters killing anyone, terrorists killing Jews, movies portraying abuse of women as romance, parents selling their children, corporations betraying generations of trust, politicians lying for votes, preoccupation with sex, pedophiles preying on our children, men becoming women, women kept as sex slaves in a basement prison, obsession with entertainers, students bullying students who kill themselves to escape the emotional pain, social media destroying reputations,

cyber thefts of identity, teachers seducing their students, babies
aborted as a means of birth control . . . aborted baby parts sold to
the highest bidder . . . we "have become filled with every kind
of wickedness, evil, greed, and depravity. [We] are full of envy,
murder, strife, deceit and malice. [We] are gossips, slanderers,
God-haters, insolent, arrogant and boastful; [we] invent ways of
doing evil; [we] disobey [our] parents; [we] are senseless, faithless,
heartless . . ."[13] All of the above are signs that our beloved nation
is under the judgment of a holy, righteous God.

It's time to repent.

If we refuse to repent, and we continue rejecting God and His
moral standard, substituting our own, we reach the farthest point
away from God and the deepest stage of judgment when we "not
only continue to do these very things but also approve of those
who practice them."[14] Could this be an indirect reference to the
booming, multi-billion dollar pornography industry?

Like creeping black mold, it is poisoning hearts and homes
and hopes and health. It is insidious as it draws the viewer into
more and more deviant desires and behavior until the appetite for
perversion becomes insatiable. It nurtures sexual predators who
have become a monstrous scourge on our society, threatening
the safety of our children and young people in schools, on play-
grounds, on sidewalks, and even in the yards and the bedrooms of
our own homes.

It's time to repent.

The prophet Joel, speaking to God's people in the last
days before God's judgment fell when the enemy swept in and
destroyed everything, gave these encouraging words: "Rend your
heart and not your garments. Return to the LORD your God, for
he is gracious and compassionate, slow to anger and abounding in

love, and he relents from sending calamity. Who knows? He may turn and have pity and leave behind a blessing . . ."[15]

The good news is that God truly loves you and me. He is always on the side of His children—Jews, Gentiles, Palestinians, Americans—whoever will come to Him by way of the Cross through faith in Jesus Christ. Wherever we live. Whatever our previous backgrounds. If, as His children, we stand in the gap—on our knees—for our nation, there is still hope.

As our nation demands that God get out, He will . . .but by degrees. He backs away slowly. At any stage if our nation turns to Him in repentance of sin, we can be restored in a right relationship with Him. He would immediately halt His judgment. He would bless our nation once again. The antidote to this progressive judgment and abandonment by God is to draw near to Him and He will draw near to us.[16]

But if we do not repent, then one stage of judgment gives way to the next so that sin takes hold and it becomes less and less likely that we will turn to Him. In the end, we can be so far away from God that it's as though we've passed the tipping point. Our hearts grow so spiritually hard and callous that we plunge right into the abyss of personal and national destruction.

Which is why it's time to pray the Daniel Prayer with sincere, heartfelt confession. *Now.* Not only for our sin, but for our shame.

CONFESSION OF NATIONAL SHAME

Judah had once been steeped in the truth. She had been founded on faith in God and was birthed as a result of His promises. She had God's law, summarized by the Ten Commandments, that taught her God's standards. She had the written revelation of God, going all the way back to the beginning of time, teaching her about God's character—His faithfulness, righteousness, kindness, goodness, forgiveness—His power, purpose, patience, promises.

Judah had a written record of her own history traced through Abraham's journey, beginning when he left Ur of the Chaldeans to follow God in a life of obedient faith, entering into a covenant relationship with Him that would affect every generation thereafter, winding through the life stories of Isaac, Jacob, Joseph, and the sojourn in Egypt. She knew of God's deliverance from Egyptian bondage and oppression under the leadership of the great liberator, Moses. She knew of His miraculous care for her in the wilderness for forty years, feeding her with manna from Heaven and water from a rock, leading her with a cloudy pillar to keep her cool by day and a fiery pillar to keep her warm at night. She knew of His power to overcome her enemies, beginning with the enemy stronghold of Jericho, so that she could possess the land He had promised. She knew of His faithfulness to raise up judges and priests and prophets and kings who had led her and ruled her and taught her and protected her and provided for her.

God Himself likened Judah to a prize vineyard. He described digging up the earth, clearing it of stones, then planting it with the choicest of vines. But when He "looked for a crop of good grapes, . . . it yielded only bad fruit."

I can hear the tears choking His voice as He said, "What more could have been done for my vineyard than I have done for it?"[17] He had done everything for her, only to be rejected.

In the bright light of truth and all that Judah had known and been taught, she had thrown away God's moral standard, substituted her own, and defiantly insisted on her "right" to do as she pleased. But God's love is so great, He does not give up easily. So He had sent Isaiah to speak to her with moving eloquence. He had sent Jeremiah to warn her with passionate tears. He had sent Amos to preach with practical logic. He had sent Ezekiel who had revealed signs and wonders. But Judah did not listen. Judah *would not* listen and that was shameful because she knew better: "We have not listened to your servants the prophets . . . this day we are covered with shame . . . O LORD, we and our kings, our princes and our fathers are covered with shame because we have sinned against you" (9:6, 7, 8).

Even when warned by powerful prophetic voices such as that of Jeremiah and Isaiah who had turned on the light of God's truth, she had stubbornly persisted in her sin. She had insisted on rejecting Him and turning to other gods. So finally, God let her go. He allowed the Babylonians to come in and have their way. For sixty-seven years she had been taught a hard lesson, that God does not tolerate wrongdoing, wickedness, and willfulness on the part of His people. If we reject Him, we will be rejected by Him.[18]

As I observe our nation today, I see the light of God's truth going forth in many different ways and in many different forms. But His light can hurt the "eyes" of those who live in the darkness, offending them with the truth of their moral condition. As a result, they cringe, pull back, and withdraw from it . . . or they seek to turn it off.

Today in our nation, people are trying to turn off the light by removing the name of God from the Pledge of Allegiance, changing the name of Christmas to Winter Holiday, blurring the distinction of who God is by insisting we all worship the same god, refusing to allow military chaplains to pray in the name of Jesus, ridiculing anyone who takes the Bible literally . . . or

believes that in the beginning God created everything . . . or says
Jesus is the only way to Heaven . . . and on and on.

CONFESSION OF SHAME FOR THE CHURCH

Even within churches, we can see a moral "twilight" and
encroaching darkness. Entire denominations have turned off the
light by denying that Jesus is the only way to God . . . that the
Bible is God's infallible, inerrant, inspired Word . . . that there is
a hell and there is a Heaven . . . and the list could go on. Sin is
either rationalized, denied, or covered up.

This was brought home to me not too long ago, when I was
invited to speak in a fast-growing megachurch led by a dynamic
young pastor. The church was being filled in multiple services
by many people who were attending for the first time. While I
assumed regular attenders and members heard good preaching on
a weekly basis, I wondered if they—along with the many first-
time visitors—had placed their faith in Jesus Christ as their own
personal Savior.

Since the young pastor had given me the freedom to speak
on any subject I chose, I felt God led me to present the Gospel
as clearly and as winsomely as I could. So at each of the multiple
Sunday morning worship services that's just what I did; however,
the congregation did not seem responsive. As I wondered why,
the reason emerged from the pastor's response at the conclusion
of the morning. With a grim tone, he remarked, "Anne, we don't
talk about judgment here."

His comment took me by surprise. It caught me up short as
thoughts began swirling around in my head: *Is that why his church
is growing so fast? Is that why he's so popular? Is he giving these people*

warm, funny, practical, caring, biblical sermons that lack the whole truth? When God's Word is unpleasant, uncomfortable, unpopular, is it also unspoken? I could almost hear the "click" of the switch as the light was turned off.

Church leaders can give the impression that they have a greater desire to have large congregations, to be popular, accepted, and successful, to be published authors or radio personalities or conference speakers than they do to hold up the Truth. They seem to care more about their own reputations and the favorable opinion of the general public than God's opinion.

When did pastors stop being shepherds and become CEOs? When did ministry leaders become celebrities? When did gifted ministries become big business that charge fees for their services? When did Christian speakers start manipulating the emotions of their audiences to attract people to themselves instead of pointing them to Jesus? When was the Gospel message of sin, salvation, and the Savior replaced with a message of health, wealth, and prosperity? I don't know, but it must make Heaven weep.

It's shameful.

I'll never forget my conversation with a man who had been a religion editor for a major newspaper. He said he had placed his faith in Jesus as his Savior. He had joined a Bible study, made Christian friends, and attended church. But within a few years, he gradually had become convinced that he had been deceived. He ended up totally rejecting Jesus and everything to do with Him and became an outspoken agnostic. The reason? The hypocrisy he had seen within the church.

He went so far in the conversation as to name specifics, then concluded in words something like this, "Anne, I have seen no difference in the behavior of those inside the church than with those outside the church. It's just that outside the church we don't pretend to be righteous." I honestly wish I could have said I didn't know what he was talking about. But I did.

If a church leader is exposed as a pedophile, the denomination quietly moves him to another location. If he is exposed as an adulterer, he may be removed, but then his behavior is excused as an addiction, and he gains acceptance with another congregation. If an individual believer is wealthy and powerful, his sin is quickly rationalized and the person is catered to because of his philanthropy. If the sin is accepted and legalized by society, then the sinner may be ordained and even given a church pulpit. Couples living in sin are given the blessing of the church.

It's shameful.

It's also dangerous. When the church either dims the light of God's Truth, or turns the Light off altogether, the nation begins operating and functioning in spiritual darkness. There is no moral, spiritual compass to warn when the nation loses its way and is in danger of self-destructing. There is no guiding light to show the nation how to get back on the right path.

In North Carolina, our rugged coast has been nicknamed the Graveyard of the Atlantic because so many ships have come to ruin on our treacherous Outer Banks. So our shoreline remains dotted with lighthouses. Whether the lighthouse is located on a sheer rock-faced cliff, a beautiful white sandy beach, or at the entrance to a harbor, the purpose of each one is to help ships find their way safely in the dark. Without them, ships have to guess their way through dangerous waters and currents. Many ships, although navigating to the best of their ability without the light, have run aground on the submerged rocks and been shattered by the pounding waves.[19]

One can imagine what would happen if there was no light illuminating safe passage from the shore. Ships would founder in the hostile, changing sea. Some vessels might make it through, but others would wind up wrecked on the shoreline. They would end as tragic statistics of the consequence of a lighthouse that may have been on the shore, but whose light was ineffective because it was nonfunctioning or too dim to make a difference.

The church in many real ways is intended to be the spiritual lighthouse of a nation. The apostle Paul, writing to a young pastor, confirmed, "the church of the living God [is] the pillar and foundation of the truth."[20] When the church functions in the healthy way Paul described it, it clearly and consistently proclaims the truth, serving as a moral compass, warning when a nation veers from a safe course. It also is a guiding light that shows a nation how to return to the right path. But if the light has grown dim through compromise or turned off altogether, then the nation increasingly founders in the stormy seas of moral and spiritual relativism and bankruptcy.

The church should be vibrant and alive, a clear, powerful beacon of truth and hope that directs a nation to the right way. We have everything we need to be a strong, spiritual lighthouse. Added to the Old Testament revelation, we also have the New Testament. We have the completed canon of Scripture available not just in the poetic but unfamiliar language of King James, but in modern, easy-to-read and easy-to-understand translations. Bibles now have notes on almost every page to explain difficult passages and give background information and context.

Living after Pentecost, we have the indwelling of the Holy Spirit who teaches us from the inside out what it is to be a follower of Jesus Christ. His Spirit then gives us the power to live in such a way that we ourselves are small lighthouses pointing the way to Jesus by the way we live and by what we say.

In addition, we have over two thousand years of church history. God has sent preachers and teachers and prophets. Not only do we have those whose words are recorded in our Bibles, but God has given us the insight and wisdom from generations of godly men such as Ambrose, Augustine, Anselm, John Wycliffe, John Huss, Martin Luther, John Calvin, John Knox, John Bunyan, Jonathan Edwards, John Wesley, George Whitefield, Francis Asbury, William Carey, Charles Haddon Spurgeon, Dwight L. Moody, I. M. Haldeman, Billy Sunday, and Billy Graham. Men who not only publicly spoke the truth but lived the truth behind closed doors.

Today, through radio, the internet, and television, as well as through books, magazines, and the printed page, God has sent us enough great teachers and preachers who powerfully present the truth and how to live by it so that we are without excuse. Are people listening? Are people responding? Is our nation seeking God? Are we becoming more righteous and blessed?

No?! That's *shameful!*

When sending out His disciples to tell others that "the kingdom of heaven is near," Jesus had warned that if any town refused to receive them, "it will be more bearable for Sodom and Gomorrah on the day of judgment than for that town."[21] It makes me cringe to think of what He would say today to His disciples as He sends us out into the schools, the businesses, the marketplace, the neighborhoods, the halls of government, the inner cities, the suburbs, the shopping malls, to tell others that the King has come! And He is coming again!

What would Jesus say when instead of being welcomed and gladly received, we are rejected, ostracized, persecuted, demoted, ridiculed, and marginalized? With my mother's characteristic ability to say a lot in a few words, she warned of what she knew He would say when she remarked that if God doesn't judge our nation, He will need to apologize to Sodom and Gomorrah. Because, while Sodom and Gomorrah were exceedingly wicked, they only had a small glimmer of light, while on the other hand, we have had a lot of light fully revealed.

The sinful, shameful condition of our nation today and the church within her borders is not only scorned in Heaven, but brings scorn to the name of God on earth.

PERSONAL CONFESSION FOR GLOBAL SCORN

I wonder if Judah's sin and shame had so gripped Daniel's heart that with a voice choking in emotion he blurted out what he felt was the worst consequence of all. Still including himself as he used plural pronouns, he painfully acknowledged: "Our sins and . . . iniquities . . . have made . . . your people an object of scorn to all those around us" (9:16).

The nations of the world looked at God's people and saw them in captivity. Their houses were desolate. Their cities were devastated. Their temple was destroyed. If their God was anywhere around, there was no evidence of Him or of His power or of His protection or of His blessing. Which led the nations to conclude that Judah's God was not God after all.

Or if He was God, He was not supreme and could be conquered and rendered impotent by others. And so His Name was held in derision—scorned because of Judah's sin.

Rather than exclusively applying this to our nation, which seems to no longer be identified as Christian, it may be clearer to see the parallel with the church and with individual believers. Because every time a church leader is caught in sexual immorality—every time a Christian is caught lying or cheating—every time a crime is committed by a church deacon or elder—every time it is *God's Name* that is derided.

Our sinful behavior makes a mockery of who He is to the world around us. Instead of looking at us and seeing a reflection of Jesus, the world looks at us and sees a reflection of themselves. We are seen to live as practical atheists who say we believe in God but act and speak as though He doesn't exist, which leads the world to dismiss Him as irrelevant and inconsequential.

So, as you and I plow up the fallow ground of our hearts, we would do well to ask ourselves some searching questions:

Who has rejected God because of my behavior or conversation?

Am I driving people away from Him or drawing them to Him by my behavior and attitude?

Does the Light in my life shine so that others look at my character and my conduct and give genuine praise and thanks to the One who lives within me . . .

Or is the Light so dim that they don't even notice any difference between myself and them?

If all the churches in this nation were like me, would they be strong, vibrant Lighthouses pointing people to safety . . .

Or would they be to blame for the spiritual and moral darkness that has swept across our land?

If you and I want to ignite a raging fire of revival in our nation—if we want to unleash an outpouring of God's Spirit in a Third Great Awakening—then the Daniel Prayer—and the example of its author—makes it clear we must begin with wet eyes, bent knees, and a broken heart . . . for our own sin.

6

PLEADING WITH CLARITY

The first pair of binoculars I ever used belonged to my daddy. They were large, heavy, and black. He kept them in a big brown-leather case, and I had to handle them carefully so as not to drop or damage them. I remember looking through them to be the first to spot the Indigo Bunting, a small bird that returned to our house every year. His appearance signaled the beginning of summer, and so it was much anticipated.

The little bird would make his presence known by the unique tune he sang while perched precariously on the very top of the maple tree below the rail fence in our front yard. He was so small that to my naked eye he looked like a black speck. When I first spotted him in the early summer, I would run get Daddy's binoculars to verify the Indigo Bunting had returned.

However, when I first looked through the binoculars in his direction, everything would be blurred and out of focus: trees, leaves, mountains, sky, clouds all seemed to run together like a disoriented kaleidoscope. So holding the heavy binoculars as still as I could while adjusting the ring between the two eyepieces, I would see him gradually come into sharp focus—a small, bright blue bird with black wings, swaying in the breeze on the top of the tree, heralding summer with his lilting tune.

Sometimes my prayers remind me of those binoculars. Occasionally when I've begun to pray, my vision seems blurred.

Fuzzy. As though my prayer is out of focus because I don't know exactly what to pray for or how to pray. But like adjusting the focus on the binoculars while I looked through them, I've found that as I pray, my thoughts become clearer, my focus sharper, and my requests more specific.

In fact, while writing this chapter I've had two opportunities within forty-eight hours to experience this fresh clarity in prayer. The first opportunity occurred when I received a text on my cell phone from a friend. I could never remember receiving a text from her before this one. Her message was somewhat jumbled. And when I read the text, I understood why because the words had poured forth from her heart.

Her beloved husband had just gone through open-heart surgery to remove damage done by an infection. Without really thinking, I picked up my phone and called her. She answered from her husband's hospital room. After a few words of greeting, I asked if I could pray with her over the phone and she readily agreed. As I began, I had no idea what to pray for or how to enter into what they were experiencing, but I knew God knew and that as I prayed, He would give me the words. And He did. I found myself praying that the doctors would have God's wisdom in addition to their professional skill, that my dear friend would have His peace, and that her husband would be restored to health. My friend shared later that my prayer and the Scripture I had offered were a comfort to them both.

The second opportunity developed as my daughter was leaving our house after coming by to see my husband. She turned to say good-bye, and the look on her face let me know she needed to hear her mother praying for her. So I asked her to pause for a moment before going out the door. I slipped my arm around her and started to pray. I didn't know what to pray for, but again, I knew God knew and that He would give me the words as I prayed.

And I knew the words that flowed weren't just expressing my own ideas but were coming from the heart of her Heavenly Father. The words conveyed His love for her and His understanding of what it feels like to face difficulty, hardship, and persecution. But the words also pulsated with hope because He promised to bring her through her trial into a freshness of His glory and power. As I finished, tears trickled down her face, but her expression was much brighter. She had been ushered into her Heavenly Father's presence and felt His loving care.

I suspect Daniel must have experienced a similar revelation while praying because he alludes to the fact that God gave him insight and understanding, "While I was speaking and praying, confessing my sin and the sin of my people . . . while I was still in prayer . . ." (9:20–21). I find this encouraging that we don't have to know specifically how or what to pray in order to submit to our Father's guiding whisper. Sometimes I believe we're intimidated to pray beyond the limits of what we can imagine or understand. But God knows what's ahead and how He wants to answer and use us.

Why is it that I think after I pray it's my responsibility to do all I can to bring about the answer? Why do I take the battle into my own hands? Like a drowning person who tries to "help" the rescuer, I wonder how many times I have actually hindered God's answer to my prayers. I find it encouraging to be reassured that I don't have to know everything, understand everything, analyze everything before I pray for something.

This is true for all of us. We don't have to have a clear comprehension of what the need is or what the solution should be. We don't have to tell God how to "fix" things or even suggest what His course of action might be. We don't have to solve the problem for Him. What a relief it is to know all we have to do is to get down on our knees and state the problem. The burden to resolve the situation is His, not yours and mine.

SIMPLICITY IN PRAYER

In addition to praying when we don't know the answers, we are also free to pray without using eloquent speech or poetic phrases. The simplicity of just stating the need is beautifully illustrated by Jesus' own mother, Mary, during the wedding reception of a newly married young couple in Cana of Galilee. Jesus and His disciples had been invited, and were in attendance. However, the celebration almost ended prematurely when the wine ran out before the festivities had concluded. When Mary learned of the shortage, she took the initiative to resolve it, not wanting to see the young couple and their families embarrassed.

While the crisis doesn't seem catastrophic to us, it would have been so to the bride and groom in that day. In their culture, to run out of wine would have been considered the height of rudeness, indicating a lack of hospitality due to inadequate preparation. It could have led to the bridegroom being sued by the bride's family. At the very least the young couple would have been humiliated in the eyes of their family, friends, and neighbors. This is definitely not the way most "just married" couples want to begin their life together.[1]

Mary did not wring her hands in despair or hyperventilate in panic or try to fix the situation herself. She just went to Jesus and stated the problem, "They have no more wine."[2] What could have been simpler? She didn't struggle with how to pray or what to ask for. As His mother, she could have been tempted to tell Him what to do and how to do it. But she didn't even make a suggestion. She just stated the need.

While I don't think Mary understood all the details and ramifications of her request as it would impact the embryo of her son's public ministry, she centered her "prayer" on Jesus because she believed . . . *she knew* . . . He was not only her son, but God's Son. And she knew Him well enough to know that He would care about the crisis and do something about it. In response to His mother's simple statement, He performed the first miracle of His ministry. He turned water into wine and the crisis was averted.

We can learn much from Mary's example here. Too often when we pray, we seem to forget God already knows the details of our requests and how to respond in His infinite wisdom. This mind-set reminds me of people who go to the doctor only to tell him how to diagnose their ailment. When we are faced with a crisis in our own lives or in the lives of those we love, why do we feel we must take on the burden of figuring out what went wrong, what the state of affairs is now, and how it should be fixed?

Perhaps, like me, you've heard prayers similar to this one:

Dear God,

My cousin's mother—that's my father's brother's wife—needs your help. She's seventy years old and has really bad arthritis. The other day she was working in her vegetable garden—even at her age she still loves working outdoors. So the other day she was weeding in her bean patch, bending down, when she stumbled and fell and broke her hip—her right one. She lay there until her neighbor spotted her and called 911. Thank You, Lord, for letting her neighbor find her. So she's going to have to have surgery to replace her hip. Please heal her hip and give her doctor wisdom about how to operate . . . and also . . . and finally . . . amen.

Forgive me for exaggerating, but haven't we all heard prayers like this one? Maybe even prayed this way ourselves? We feel compelled to give God information as if He won't understand the situation or know what to do, along with detailed instructions on how to fix it!

This seems humorous when we stop to think about it, but it also reveals a superficial understanding of who God is. Because God is God! He can do anything and He knows everything. All you and I need to do is lay our burdens at His feet. Place them in His capable hands. Crawl up in His lap, put your head on His shoulder, and rest in Him. Sometimes no words are necessary. Weep if you must. He can interpret the tears.

INTENSITY IN PRAYER

I expect there may have been tears on Daniel's face as he continued to pour out his heart. As he prayed, his prayer came more clearly into focus. With almost rapid-fire intensity, he stated what he was pleading for: "Turn away your anger and your wrath from Jerusalem, your city, your holy hill . . . hear the prayers and petitions of your servant . . . look with favor on your desolate sanctuary . . . Give ear, O God, and hear; open your eyes and see . . . O Lord, listen! O Lord, forgive! O Lord, hear and act!" (9:16, 17, 18, 19).

Once again we discover that it was God's Word that compelled Daniel to pray. While he doesn't refer to a specific passage as he did earlier when he had said he was reading from the prophet Jeremiah, his prayer still reflected a promise given hundreds of years earlier when God had vowed to hear prayers offered for Jerusalem. When King Solomon had dedicated the temple, God had declared, "Now my eyes will be open and my ears attentive to the prayers offered in this place. I have chosen and consecrated this temple so that my Name may be there forever. My eyes and my heart will always be there."[3] God had promised to look on the city He loved and to always care for it.

Since Daniel had a copy of Jeremiah's writings, which he considered Scripture, I'm quite sure he also had a copy of other portions we refer to as the Old Testament, including the history of Israel, which contained the above promises given to Solomon. The conclusion of Daniel's prayer traced the promises that God had given so much earlier and had been carefully recorded in the chronicles of Israel's history. Once again Daniel was compelled to pray according to the promises in God's Word. As Daniel poured out his heart in an intense staccato of requests, he became clearer and clearer in what he was asking. Let me paraphrase Daniel's requests . . .

O God, in keeping with Your own righteous acts, hear my prayer when I cry to You. You said Your eyes would be open to prayers that are offered in the temple in Jerusalem. But, O God, there is no

Jerusalem and there is no temple there. You have poured out Your wrath on Your city. On Your holy hill. "You have fulfilled the words spoken against us and against our rulers by bringing upon us great disaster. Under the whole heaven nothing has ever been done like what has been done to Jerusalem" (9:12).

Look on the burned-out buildings, the piles of rubble, the broken-down walls, the place where You said You would place Your Name. How can I pray from there? I can only pray from here. But I hold You to Your Word, O Lord God. You said Your Name would be on Jerusalem forever. You have said Your eyes would be on her and Your heart would be there.[4]

So, O God, open Your eyes and look on Your city! Look on Jerusalem. O God, open Your ears and listen! Hear my cry. Be attentive to my prayer. Forgive us! Release us! Restore us! Revive us!

Daniel's entire prayer became intensely focused on asking God for what He wanted to give and what He had promised to give. The Daniel Prayer does not teach us to pray for what we want God to do for us or for our family or for our church or for our nation or for our world. The Daniel Prayer teaches you and me to pray until we enter into the very heart of the Father and discover what it is He wants to do for us or what He wants to give us. We discover His "wants" through the promises in His Word which the Holy Spirit will impress on our hearts.

DISCOVERY IN PRAYER

We need to pray until we can unload all we are thinking and all we want in order to get down to what God is thinking and what He wants. Then we ask Him for what we know He wants to give us. A good example is the prayer Abraham prayed for Sodom.

Abraham had felt burdened for the spiritual condition of the world around him, for the city closest to him, and for his own family members that he knew were in danger of coming under judgment. His burden had come straight from the heart of God. And how did he know the heart of God? He had spent time walking with God.

In some respects, walking with God is similar to walking with each other. Every morning that I'm home, I get up early in the morning and walk two and a half miles around a lake in a nearby park. I sometimes walk with a friend, not only for safety, but also for the fellowship. Over the years, I've worn out several walking partners. But two basic rules have stayed the same, regardless of who walks with me.

The first rule is that we must walk in the same direction. The second rule is that we must walk at the same pace. If either of those rules is not kept, then it doesn't matter how much I enjoy the other person, or how committed we are to our friendship, or how much we both need the exercise; we won't be walking together.

The same two basic rules apply to walking with God. If we want to walk with Him, we must walk in His direction, which means we must surrender the will of our lives to Him. We can't go off in our own direction, deciding our own goals and pursuing our own purposes. And we must walk at His pace, which means step-by-step obedience to His Word. And since we would have no idea what steps He is taking on a particular day, we have to read and apply His Word on a daily basis so that we can walk at His pace. One thing I have discovered is that He won't adjust His pace or direction to suit me. I have to adjust my pace and direction to His if I want to walk with Him.

Abraham walked with God. As they walked together, God had revealed that He was going to destroy Sodom and Gomorrah.[5] And so Abraham began to pray for what he knew was on God's mind and heart. He began to intercede with God for the people who were living in Sodom. His prayer revealed that he didn't know exactly what to ask for, so he just started by asking God to spare Sodom for the sake of fifty righteous people who lived there. When God agreed, Abraham's prayer progressed to asking for Sodom to be spared for forty people, then thirty people, then twenty people, then ten people. As Abraham prayed, he was learning what to pray for.

Each request Abraham made was answered by God in agreement. But after God agreed to spare Sodom for the sake of ten righteous people who lived there, God finished speaking with Abraham and then left. So Abraham went home. Abraham never voiced what I think must have been the deepest prayer of his heart, which was for his nephew Lot to be saved from judgment when it fell. But God knew.

It's encouraging to me to know I don't have to always say things exactly right when I pray. I just need to pray. And God, who searches my heart and knows the deep desires that are there, will answer in His own way.[6] God knew the real desire in Abraham's heart. So when He couldn't even find ten righteous people living in Sodom, He destroyed it. Yet remembering Abraham's prayer, God reached down and supernaturally delivered Lot and his family from His judgment.[7] Lot's salvation is what Abraham had undoubtedly wanted. And that's what God had wanted to give him when He first imparted His burden to Abraham, moving him to pray accordingly.

SENSITIVITY IN PRAYER

Like Abraham's prayer for Sodom, the Daniel Prayer is a work of God's Spirit in us and through us. As we pray, the Holy Spirit within us will direct us in what to pray for. Jesus promised His disciples that the Holy Spirit would guide them into all truth, bringing to their minds the things they needed to remember.[8] While He was certainly speaking of the anointing His disciples were given in order to record His words for you and me in what we know as the New Testament writings; while He certainly was reassuring them that when they were placed on trial for their faith they could rely on the Holy Spirit to give them answers for their interrogators; I also believe that what He said could be applied to our prayers for our families, our churches, our nation, and our world. In other words, one application of what Jesus promised was that as we pray, God the Holy Spirit would bring to our minds the Scripture on which we need to base our prayers.

We have already seen that Daniel was reading Jeremiah when he came across the promise from God that compelled him to pray. And toward the end of his prayer, he was again praying the promises of God which I believe the Holy Spirit brought to his mind. But to remind Daniel of what God had said, Daniel had to have read it at some point.

The Holy Spirit can't bring to our remembrance things we have never known. Which is one reason it's so important to read and saturate ourselves in Scripture so that it's available for the Holy Spirit to pull up from the recesses of our memories as we pray.

I shared with you that I prayed for my friend who had texted me when her husband was recuperating from open heart surgery.

As I prayed, Psalm 73:26 came to mind, which promises, "My flesh and my heart may fail, but God is the strength of my heart and my portion forever." So I claimed that promise in prayer for her husband. Within the week, he was released from the hospital to continue his recovery at home.

I also told you that I prayed for my daughter. As I prayed, the Holy Spirit brought to my attention that it was the Wednesday before Maundy Thursday. While Scripture doesn't tell us what Jesus did on that "silent" day, I was prompted to voice in prayer that surely He looked ahead with some apprehension and dread at what He knew He was facing the next day. Yet His Father not only strengthened Him for the trials, the torture, and the crucifixion, but brought Him through to the glory of the resurrection. As a result of remembering this in prayer, my daughter was reassured that Jesus understood her feelings and would strengthen her for the challenges ahead, then bring her triumphantly through them. He did!

When you pray, ask the Holy Spirit to teach you how to pray. And what to pray. Take your Bible into your place of prayer. As you read it, open your heart and mind to His still, small voice that will whisper in your "ear" and give direction to your thoughts and words.[9] In prayer, be sensitive to Him.

PRIORITY IN PRAYER

The last words recorded in the Daniel Prayer are, "O Lord, listen! O Lord, forgive! O Lord, hear and act!" *Why? What was the basic reason for his entire prayer?* "For your sake, O my God, do not delay, because your city and your people bear your Name" (9:19). There it is! Like a nugget of gold gleaming in the stream of his prayer, Daniel came to the bottom line.

Having pleaded with confidence in God's character and in God's covenant; having acknowledged that his people had spurned repeated warnings God had sent and therefore deserved the judgment they had received; having pleaded with fasting, in sackcloth and ashes, in honest and humble confession of sin and shame and scorn; having voiced his desperation for God to make good on His promise given through Jeremiah to set his people free after seventy years of captivity, Daniel stated very simply and succinctly what his prayer was all about. It was a heartfelt plea for God to be glorified in His city and in His people for His own great Name's sake. His entire prayer became focused on asking God for what He wanted to give.

And therein lies the secret to the Daniel Prayer.

Regardless of whether or not Daniel had humbled himself enough . . .

Regardless of whether or not Daniel had fasted long enough . . .

Regardless of whether or not Daniel's confession had been thorough enough . . .

Regardless of whether or not Daniel had claimed Scripture enough . . .

Bottom line, Daniel's priority in prayer was that God's Name be cleared. Exalted. Glorified. That the shame brought to it by the behavior of His people and the subsequent judgment would be cleansed as God kept His promise to release them from captivity and restore them to His place of blessing. Daniel longed for the nations of the world to recognize that Israel's God is God. He longed for the world to acknowledge that his God is indeed faithful and gracious and good and great.

As you pray, what is your heartfelt priority?

Relief from pain?

Reconciliation of a relationship?

Restoration of health?

Resolution of financial issues?

Recognition of your profile?

Reinstatement to your job?

Removal of an enemy?

Repression of gossip?

Rescue from trouble?

Reward for well-doing?

I've prayed all of the above, and more. But while free to pour out my heart and tell God what I want, underneath the requests and overarching them all is the priority of God's glory. I long for God's Name to be exalted through the way my prayer is, *or is not*, answered. And that's the clear bottom line of the Daniel Prayer.

So . . . in our world . . .

> Where 148 Christian students were gunned down by Islamic terrorists, and the slaughter barely made mainline news . . .
>
> Where 21 Christian men were marched along a beach and beheaded for a terrorist recruiting video . . .
>
> Where businesses have been forced to close because the owners stand by their religious convictions . . .
>
> Where Israel has been portrayed as the villain, and the surrounding nations who send in suicide bombers and

missiles to terrorize the Jews have been portrayed as the victims . . .

Where a Protestant minister proudly declared he doesn't believe in God and that what we know of Jesus is a legend, yet resents being told he's not a Christian . . .[10]

Where a young racist enters a church, sits in on the prayer meeting and Bible study for an hour, then pulls out a gun and murders the pastor and eight others . . .

Where the flames of racial hatred have been fanned by lies and distortions to keep us divided . . .

Where sex acts are simulated for entertainment . . .

Where the poor and oppressed are used for political advantage . . .

When unborn babies are aborted, their beating hearts preserved so that their body parts can be sold . . .

In our world . . .

I long to see the sky unfold and a Rider appear
whose Name is Faithful and True . . .[11]

I long to see the Lamb of God return as the Lion of Judah
followed by the armies of Heaven . .[12]

I long to hear the universe erupt in acclamation
of the One who alone is worthy to receive
power and wealth and wisdom and strength and honor
and glory and praise . . .[13]

I long . . .

for truth to triumph over lies,
for love to triumph over hate,

for peace to triumph over war,

for right to triumph over wrong,

for good to triumph over evil . . .

I long for the world, at long last, to be ruled rightly with justice and mercy and truth and love and peace.

I long for every eye to see, and for every knee to bow, and for every tongue to confess that Jesus Christ is . . .

The Prince of Peace,

the Son of God,

the Son of Man,

the Messiah of Israel,

the Creator who became our Savior,

the Lord of lords and the King of kings . . .

to the glory of God the Father![14]

I long for the world to see Jesus as He truly is.

Come, Lord Jesus! Reveal Yourself in power and glory and majesty and authority to this wicked, sinful, rebellious world that You love. That You died to redeem. That You have purchased for Yourself. Show them who You are. For the glory of Your Name.

PART THREE

PREVAILING
IN PRAYER

*I have heard
the prayer and plea
you have made before me.*

1 KINGS 9:3

ANSWERED IMMEDIATELY

When Danny and I would first sit down to eat our dinner, our Golden Retriever Wilbur would race over to Danny and, with an excited grin on his face, let Danny know he wanted some scraps of food. If allowed, he would have jumped up on Danny, insisting on something from his plate. But I would not allow him to beg at the table. So when we began to eat, Wilbur sat beside Danny, looking soulfully at the food. We both knew exactly what he wanted. Then after a few minutes Wilbur would rest his head in Danny's lap, rolling his big brown eyes toward the plate. Invariably, he got something because Danny couldn't resist those loving, longing eyes.

Like Wilbur, once I articulate what it is that I'm asking God for, once I have Scripture to confirm that what I am asking Him to give me is what He also wants me to receive, once I'm confident He has heard my prayer, I don't have to keep begging. I know He knows. And how do I know He has heard and will answer? Because the burden in my heart will lift. I will feel released from it. In fact, I will keep praying until I am released from the burden, and then I transition into the waiting mode. Even as I pray about other things or get on to the business of my day, my spirit remains in a position of waiting. It's as though I have placed "my head in His lap," reminding Him that I'm here and I'm still waiting to receive His answer.

Throughout history, God has honored the prevailing prayers of His people. In the first century BC, the unmistakable sound of the shofar could be heard coming from the wall surrounding Jerusalem, echoing across the sun-scorched valley. The blowing of the trumpet heralded great public distress and was used to summon the people. A severe drought was threatening the very existence of Jerusalem. And so the city elders called for the people to gather outside the city walls. Then they sent for Honi, an old man known for his devout faith.

After he was summoned, the elders asked Honi, "Pray that rain may fall." Honi prayed but nothing happened. So he drew a circle around himself in the dust of the ground and prayed again, "O Lord of the world, Your children have turned their faces to me . . . I swear by Your great name that I will not stir from here until You have pity on Your children."

The rain began to fall, one large drop at a time. But Honi protested, "Not for such rain have I prayed, but for rain that will fill the cisterns, pits, and caverns."

In answer to his prayer, the heavens opened and the waters descended in a violent gully washer that threatened to flood the city. So once again, Honi pleaded, "Not for such rain have I prayed, but for rain of goodwill, blessing and graciousness." It is said, and recorded by the Jewish historian Josephus, that in response to Honi's third prayer, a long, soaking rain began to fall that ended the three-year drought.[1] Honi had prevailed in prayer and became known as the Circle Maker.

Hundreds of years before Honi, Elijah had challenged the wicked, idolatrous priests of Baal to a contest that would reveal once and for all to the people whose god was God. When Baal remained silent and still as his priests screamed, danced, and slashed themselves to get his attention, Elijah stepped up and told them they had had their chance. Now it was his turn. When Elijah called on his God—the God of Abraham, Isaac, and Israel—the fire fell! In full view of all the priests and the people, the fire consumed the sacrifice. The priests of Baal were exposed for their religious hypocrisy. They were defeated and the people shouted their acknowledgment, "The Lord—he is God! The Lord—he is God!"

But Elijah knew his work was not done. God had promised him that if he would confront the wicked King Ahab and the priests of Baal, then God would end the three-year drought Israel was experiencing. So Elijah climbed back up on Mt. Carmel, crouched down with his face to the ground, and prayed for rain. It didn't come. So he prayed again. It didn't come. He prayed again. And again. And again. And again. And again. He prayed seven times! Finally a small cloud was spotted that signaled God's answer. Before Elijah could get to cover, the rain began to pour down.[2] Elijah had prevailed in prayer.

Hundreds of years before Elijah, Abraham's grandson Jacob was returning to Canaan after twenty years in exile. His intention was to claim the birthright that he had bought from his brother, Esau, and stolen from his father, Isaac. When he came to the border of the land promised to him which was marked by the Jabbok River, he sent his family, his livestock, and his servants on ahead of him.

It was evening when he stepped out to follow them. But his way was blocked by a Man who would not let him pass. Jacob then wrestled with the Man all night, refusing to give in or give up. Finally the Man broke Jacob's hip. But instead of crumbling at the Man's feet and whimpering in defeat and self-pity, Jacob wound his arms around the Man's neck and said he would not let go until the Man blessed him. And who was the Man? He was none other than the Lord God. He then blessed Jacob there.[3] Jacob had prevailed in prayer.

What does it mean to prevail in prayer? Simply put, it means to persevere until you receive the answer. It means to draw a "circle" around yourself in the dust, and refuse to leave until God sends the "rain." It means to stay on your face and refuse to settle for less than everything God has promised. It means to put your arms of faith about your Father's neck and cling tightly to Him until He blesses you. But to prevail, you must be sure that what you are praying for is something you know God wants to give you. And how do you know what He wants to give you? You base your prayer on God's Word. Then you hold Him to it through prevailing prayer.

While prevailing prayer doesn't necessarily mean that you literally draw a circle or stay in a place of prayer 24/7, it does mean that your spirit holds a position of prayer before God until an answer is given. It means you wrap your heart and mind around whatever it is you are asking of God until He answers. On the one hand, if we keep repeating the same prayer over and over, it implies we lack the faith to believe God has heard and that He will answer. On the other hand, having prayed once, we can't just walk away from it until it's answered. We need to pray like Elijah—praying repeatedly until we have the assurance God has heard and will answer—then we thank Him by faith for the answer even before it comes, and rise up from our knees.

Daniel didn't have to wait long before he received the immediate assurance that God had heard his prayer. He had pleaded with laser-focused confidence, with heartrending confession, and with pinpoint clarity. Even before he finished praying, his burden was lifted when he received an answer that came by special delivery: "While I was still in prayer, Gabriel . . . instructed me and said to me, 'Daniel . . . As soon as you began to pray, an answer was given, which I have come to tell you, for you are highly esteemed'" (9:21–23). *His prayer had moved Heaven!*

The incredible revelation was that Heaven was moved as soon as Daniel began to pray! God didn't wait to see how long Daniel would hold out in his fasting. God didn't wait to see how long Daniel would leave the ashes smeared on his face or the tattered rags on his body. The Daniel Prayer is not a legalistic exercise where you and I prove to God we are somehow spiritual enough, worthy enough, humble enough, desperate enough, sincere enough to earn an answer.

God looks on the heart of the one who is praying. He is moved by our trust in Him. Trust in Him alone. He is not an "add-on" God. As we pray we cannot have several options up our sleeve. We can't have a Plan A, and if that doesn't work a Plan B, then we tack prayer on as though God is our fallback plan.

The Daniel Prayer is a prayer that is wholly, totally, exclusively centered on God. We pray absolutely convinced that if God does not come through for us, we won't come through. That if He doesn't help us, we won't be helped. If He doesn't save us, we're doomed. But for those who put their trust in Him and Him alone, they discover He is the God of the impossible who finds great delight in revealing His power to make a way where there is no way. He is a God of miracles who also loves to encourage us in prayer.

IMMEDIATELY ENCOURAGED BY THE ANSWER

How wonderful would it be if, as we were praying, an angel would show up with the answer to our prayer! While I almost envy the way Daniel received his answer, in my experience that has never happened. But I have received answers to prayer from God's appointed "messengers."

One messenger stands out in my mind because the answer he gave was a dramatic turning point for me during a very difficult time. Several years ago in my ministry, I uncovered a full-time staff person who was simultaneously working on another job. When I confronted her with it, she became irate, accused me of lying, insisted she was entitled to supplement her income, and appealed over my head to the ministry's board of directors. After hearing her thoroughly state her case, the board unanimously recommended that she be terminated. Which she was. Although she had entered into a signed covenant with the other two ministry directors, when she left they pledged to stay. However, two weeks after her termination, they both turned in their resignations.

Suddenly I was left with a ministry that was facing four major national and international initiatives within the next nine months but without the directors who would have helped me accomplish them. To say I prayed is an understatement. I was launched into that stratosphere of faith where God—and God alone—was my refuge and strength. I was wholly centered on Him, knowing beyond a shadow of a doubt that if He did not help me, I would not be helped and my ministry would collapse.

Within twenty-four hours God sent His messenger to me with an immediate answer. The messenger was the husband of one of my board members. I was attending a meeting that just "happened" to have been previously scheduled for the day after I had learned of the mass exodus of directors from my ministry. My board member and her husband, Vicki and Ray Bentley, were also among others at the meeting. The three of us had just finished discussing my situation when we walked from lunch to the next conference seminar.

As we walked through the hotel corridor, they told me they had just been to Mount Vernon, the home place of President Washington. My head was spinning, and I thought, "What does that have to do with the situation I'm in?" But I listened. Ray went on to say that he loved George Washington and that one thing he had learned was that he should never have won the Revolutionary War. But he did win because God had brought him great generals who had helped him. Then Ray stopped me, put his hands on my shoulders so that I had to look him directly in the eye, and delivered the initial answer to my prayer. "Anne, God will bring you generals."

Deep in my heart, the burden was lifted. *I knew* God had heard my prayer and would bring me through. I assure you that I maintained a position of prayer in my heart while I continued to wait for the specific answers, but God's peace that defies all practical logic flooded my heart and never left. I was greatly encouraged by the "insight and understanding" that God had heard my prayer and would indeed bring me through.

IMMEDIATELY ENCOURAGED BY THE AFFIRMATION

Daniel too knew God would see him through. The very fact that Gabriel had been sent by God to give Daniel a message must have immediately relieved the burden that weighed so heavily on Daniel's heart. Until that moment, Daniel would not have known for sure if he had interpreted Jeremiah's prophecy accurately. He would not have known for sure if he had been praying appropriately. He would not have known without a doubt if anyone was listening or caring or heeding or moving in response to his prayer.

So not only must Gabriel's message have relieved Daniel's burden as it conveyed that God had heard, but it affirmed Daniel personally when Gabriel revealed, "Daniel . . . you are highly esteemed" (9:22–23). How those five words must have thrilled him. To know that God not only noticed Daniel, but that He knew Daniel by name. To know that God not only was moved by Daniel's prayer, but that the God of the Universe—the Almighty Creator—the Jehovah of Abraham, Isaac, and Jacob—the great I AM of Moses—the living God—held him in high esteem. What an amazing revelation for an old man, isolated in an upstairs room, enslaved in a foreign land, who had been pouring out his heart as he interceded with God for his nation and his people.

This affirmation is something for you and me to wrap our hearts and minds around as we consider praying the Daniel Prayer. If there was no other reward for prayer than earning Heaven's high regard, wouldn't that be enough?

> What difference would it make if our employer doesn't notice us?
>
> What difference would it make if our spouse doesn't love us?
>
> What difference would it make if our children don't thank us?
>
> What difference would it make if we don't have a spouse or a child?

What difference would it make if our parents
disinherit us?

What difference would it make if our world doesn't
honor us?

What difference would it make if we don't achieve our
own goals?

What difference would it make if our pastor doesn't
visit us?

What difference would it make if we don't have a college
degree?

What difference would it make if we are never
wealthy . . . or healthy?

What difference would it make as long as you and I have Heaven's
blessing and approval and affirmation and high esteem? When
everything is said and done, nothing else really matters, does it?

While the items on the above list can cause pain and heartache, none of them need interfere with or hinder us from
receiving God's blessing. You and I are to live for God's glory
and His pleasure. Nothing more and nothing less. It's possible to
be despised by the world while at the very same time to be held
in high esteem in Heaven. The opposite of that is also true. It's
possible to be held in high esteem on earth while being of no
consequence at all in Heaven. Think about it. Which are you?

If you enter into the Daniel Prayer, seeking to move Heaven
and change nations, you will be a person who is highly esteemed
by God. That's more than encouraging! That's exhilarating!
That's thrilling! It makes all of the fasting and ashes and rags and
hours spent in prayer more than worth it a hundred times over!

But God will also bring into your life visible people who will affirm you and bless you. As I went through the months of turmoil and tumult in my ministry, God poured out His blessing on the rest of my ministry staff who rallied around me with prayer, love, and hard work. Our initiatives were all completed with excellence, to the glory of God! And my board of directors stood by with strong words of exhortation, encouragement, and unwavering support. One by one, God brought me His generals. New staff members who were not only incredibly qualified, but also had humble, servants' hearts. My ministry thrived, and continues to thrive as we remain focused on Him, filled with His Spirit, and fired up to do the work He assigns us.

IMMEDIATELY ENLIGHTENED

Daniel was not only given the highest praise, but additionally Gabriel revealed, "I have now come to give you insight and understanding" (9:22). As noted earlier, Daniel learned how to pray and what to pray for as he prayed. Prayer is almost like a flower that begins as a tightly closed bud but then blossoms into fullness as we pray, taking on shape and a more focused aim as God brings promises from His Word to our minds that apply and brings messengers who affirm us.

Sometimes my prayers are tightly closed as I begin them because I am in a panic mode. Desperation causes me to see only one way to pray, and it usually is something like, "Get me out of this! Deliver me!" As my spirit lies prostrate before God, I plead with Him to rescue me. I wrestle and struggle and receive nothing but silence. So in the silence, when I find myself still prostrate and still pleading, I begin to settle down in my spirit. As

I deliberately calm myself and choose to obey His command not to be afraid, my spiritual fingers relax around my tightly clasped demand and I begin to let go of what I think I have to have and when I have to have it.

A few years ago I was looking forward to leading our *Just Give Me Jesus* revival in a city that had had more than their share of challenges. The local team of women had faithfully persevered, and we were all expectant of the blessing God was going to give because the battle had been intense. Four weeks before the revival, the doctor informed me that I needed to have immediate emergency abdominal surgery for diverticulitis.

He assured me I would be strong enough in a month's time to lead the revival. I felt I had no choice but to comply, and the discovery that my colon had been abscessed confirmed I had made the right choice. But my recovery was complicated by a severe case of vertigo. I could barely stand without weaving because of the disorientation caused by the dizziness. So with the vertigo added to the physical pain and weakness from the surgery, panic set in. That's when I began to demand that God do something. Now. Or at least do something by the time I left home to go to the city of the revival. Heal me. Remove the vertigo. But all I "heard" in response was silence.

I reminded God, as though He had forgotten, that the platform I used in our revivals was a round platform, centered in the middle of the arena, anchored by a podium in the shape of an old wooden cross. Once I was on it, there would be no place to hide. There would be nothing to sit down on and nothing to cling to. Except the Cross. There had been previous times when I was healthy and strong that just walking around the platform itself, looking at the silhouetted audience through the brilliant video lights, had made me light-headed. How could I handle that same situation in my present weakened, dizzy condition?

Three times in my ministry I have collapsed when in the pulpit. So I know from firsthand experience that it's a miserable, undesirable experience for everyone—for me, for the audience, and for the hosts. I was utterly convinced I was going to collapse on the platform at *Just Give Me Jesus*. I was so convinced I was going to go down that I instructed Fernando Ortega, who leads worship at the revivals, to be prepared with a few appropriate songs to cover the awkward and frightening moments when I did collapse.

As I continued to desperately pray and nothing happened, I could "feel" my spiritual fingers losing their grip on my demand. Finally, I let go. I told the Lord if my collapse would in some way bring Him glory, if He wanted to use a public display of my weakness to break through and break down the barriers so that real revival would take place, I *was* willing for that to happen. And I was willing, even though I was filled with dread.

The next morning, after I surrendered my demand for miraculous healing and deliverance, God "enlightened" me. I was sitting at my computer, with my Bible open as I worked on the notes for one of the messages, when my eye fell on Psalm 46:5 . . . "God is within her, she will not fall; God will help her at break of day." That verse pulsated with life! To this day, it still reverberates with the sound of His voice. I could almost hear Him audibly speaking to me through it.

Immediately I received enormous release from the burden I had been carrying. The very next morning as I opened one of my devotional books during my prayer time, Psalm 121:3 seemed to leap up off the page, confirming what He had said the day before . . . "He will not let your foot slip . . ." The promise was emphatic. My attitude did a 180-degree turn. I began to praise God for the strength I knew He would give to get me through my responsibilities, not just somehow, but triumphantly. I knew with certainty that I would not collapse. Because He said so.

While I certainly realize the danger of taking God's Word out of context and manipulating it so that it seems to speak personally and specifically, I also know my Shepherd's voice. After six decades of following Him, I know by experience that when I read my Bible, listening for His voice, God speaks to me personally and specifically. I've learned how to listen when He speaks to my spirit. I know this not only by experience as I have followed Him by acting on what He has said and finding that it's true and that it "works," but I also know this by faith. God's Word clearly testifies about itself that, "All Scripture is God-breathed and is useful for teaching, rebuking, correcting, and training in righteousness, so that the servant of God may be thoroughly equipped for every good work"[4] So I knew God had spoken to me and I could rely on His Word.

When I arrived in the revival city, for the first few days I was involved in media interviews and committee functions. They were carefully spaced to allow me time to rest in between so that my energy wasn't overly taxed. But as the time drew nearer for me to climb up on the platform, I began to get apprehensive once again. Although I was healing nicely from the surgery, I was still weak. And my vertigo was in full force. I can't recall how I was led to Psalm 61:2, but I know I used it to voice my fear . . . "Lord, I call as my heart grows faint; lead me to the rock that is higher than I." Once again, He immediately gave me enlightenment from Psalm 40:2, "Anne, [I] will set [your] feet on a rock and give [you] a firm place to stand. [I] will put a new song in [your] mouth, a hymn of praise to our God. Many will see and fear and put their trust in the LORD."

As I stepped up on the platform that Friday for the evening session, and again on Saturday morning for multiple sessions that would last until 5:00 that afternoon, inwardly I praised God that He was my Hiding Place and that His promises were the rock on which I would stand. He was true to His Word. My foot did not slip nor did I collapse. But He tested me.

Close to the end of the last session, I shared with the audience what I had been going through so that they would "see and fear and put their trust in the Lord." I knew better than anyone that they were glimpsing His glory, and I wanted them to "see." Their enthusiastic applause affirmed that their eyes had been opened.

Almost before I finished telling the thousands of people gathered around me about God's sustaining power and strength, the dizziness became overwhelming. My words slowed uncontrollably and I began to slur. I held onto the cross podium, and while my mouth continued to give the message, my heart was pleading in prayer, "Lord, You promised! If I go down now, the entire audience will get a different message than the one I've just given. They will see that You are not to be trusted. That You are not dependable. Lord, please, for the glory of Your Name hold me up. Let me finish. *Help me, please.*"

Once again the answer was immediate. This time it came in the form of a cool, refreshing breeze. The dizziness subsided. My words became clear. Instead of collapsing, I finished strong. When I gave the invitation to those in the arena to surrender their lives for service to Jesus, almost the entire audience stood. It was a glorious conclusion.

When the revival was over, I asked the producer if he or any of the guys in the video trucks had seen me struggling and turned on a fan to help me out. He laughed and said, "Anne, in that old arena there is no fan to turn on even if we had wanted to. No, we didn't do anything." So what had caused the breeze in an otherwise enclosed, stifling place? Was it caused by Gabriel furiously fanning his wings? Or maybe just the breath of the Holy Spirit blowing onto the platform, keeping His promise to help me and not let me fall? While I don't know where the breeze came from, I know that it came, and that God answered my prayer immediately, for the glory of His Name.

I will be the first to acknowledge that not all prayers are answered immediately with encouragement and enlightenment. When the answer is delayed, I can get discouraged and give up instead of prevailing in prayer. Which makes me wonder . . . what answers, blessings, and miracles have I missed . . .

> Because I didn't stay in the "circle" until Heaven was moved?
>
> Because I gave up after the sixth time of interceding?
>
> Because when God seemingly refused to give in to my demand, my faith collapsed and I didn't hang on until He blessed me?

So I have resolved to stay in the circle, to keep on praying, to hang on by the sheer willpower of faith until I receive what He has promised. And what has He promised for His people? "If my people, who are called by my name, will humble themselves and pray and seek my face and turn from their wicked ways, then will I hear from heaven and will forgive their sin and will heal their land."[5]

Would you share this same resolve? Drive the stake of your faith deep down into His promise. Don't quit. Don't give up. Don't give in. Don't collapse. Don't settle for less than prayer that moves Heaven and changes nations. This nation. For the glory of His Name.

8

ANSWERED ULTIMATELY

It was a typical day in Jerusalem. Like a giant brick oven, the stone streets and buildings absorbed, then reflected the heat of the sun, making it a stifling afternoon. What little breeze there may have been was blocked by the buildings and never found its way into the city center. Flies were buzzing, donkeys were braying, but the dogs were smart enough to curl up in the shade of a merchant's booth and wait until the cool of the evening before venturing out.

As the young boy made his way through the cobbled streets, he darted around vendors hawking their goods, squeezed past carts that barely made it through the narrow alleyways, and weaved his way through the crowds of shoppers purchasing their last items before heading home in the late afternoon. The smell of broiling fish, roasting lamb, and baking bread mingled with the smell of fresh animal droppings and human sweat. Permeating everything was the smell of smoke that came from the temple area. As long as he lived, his memories included not only the visuals, but the smells of the city he loved and called home.

Through the gaps of the buildings he could glimpse his destination. It was almost impossible to miss. Solomon's Temple. The pinnacle was 207 feet high. *Twenty stories.* In the sunlight, the limestone exterior gleamed until the dazzling reflection was blinding. It was situated on the highest point in the city referred to as the Holy Hill.

The boy finally arrived at the foot of the broad staircase that led up into the archways built into the wall that surrounded the temple itself. He took a deep breath of fresh air, felt the cool breeze that came up from the Kidron Valley, and looked up. From the base of the steps, he couldn't see the temple itself. His line of sight was blocked by an incredibly high wall that surrounded the entire temple area. But he knew the temple was there. So he began to climb the steps that were laid in irregular widths even though he wanted to run up them. He knew he had to pick his way carefully or he would trip and fall. So he climbed slowly. Reverently. One broad step at a time.

As the boy drew nearer to the temple area itself, he could hear the sound of the Levites singing and playing their instruments at the entrance. He could see various rituals being conducted, and gatherings of small groups of people discussing the Torah, the law of Jehovah. The area around the temple was divided into sections that were accessible to Gentiles, women, Israelite men, Levites, and priests.

Because he had come of age, he was allowed to slip inside the courtyard for Jewish men. And that's what he did. Once inside the courtyard, he knew he had drawn as near as he possibly could to the place where God was said to dwell. The place referred to as the Holy of Holies. It was in the inner recesses of the temple itself, accessible only once a year, and then only to the High Priest. But he was close. As close as he would ever get.

It was late afternoon. Then he saw it! The first tendril of smoke that lifted from the place of the evening sacrifice. It was like a gray banner waving against the cobalt blue sky, rising above the temple, reminding worshipers that their sin required a sacrifice. He knew lambs were being slain and offered on the altar for that purpose. His young heart skipped a beat. That's what he wanted. More than anything. He wanted to be free from the burden of guilt that weighed heavily on his young shoulders. He yearned to go inside the Most Holy Place until his heart ached. He wanted desperately to live in God's presence. And never leave. He was a God-worshiper . . . heart, mind, soul, and young body.

While I've used my own thoughts and imagination to sketch out the above story, memories like this surely flooded back into Daniel's mind from time to time. We know he never forgot his boyhood experience of growing up in Jerusalem, indicated by the fact that when he prayed he always opened his windows toward his beloved city. But he also would have known of the devastation caused by King Nebuchadnezzar and the Babylonian army following his capture. Not only the city of Jerusalem had been destroyed, but the temple itself had been leveled so that nothing remained. The bronze, the gold, the treasures, the artifacts—all were seized. Taken to Babylon. No one who loved and worshiped God in the temple would ever forget.

Daniel had seen with his own eyes the sacred golden vessels that had been used in temple worship of the living God used at a pagan feast for the pleasure of a spoiled, drunken Babylonian king.[1] He knew the city of Jerusalem itself was nothing but ruins. And the temple had been a pile of rubble for forty-seven years. No tendril of smoke had lifted for forty-seven years because without the temple, there had been no more sacrifices.[2]

As he prayed the Daniel Prayer, he must have been gazing out of his upstairs window, visualizing the city he had once known. We know he remembered back to the temple and the smoke rising toward Heaven. We know from his prayer that his heart was filled with longing for the day when the temple would be rebuilt. The day when the sacrifices would be reinstituted. When the streets of Jerusalem would once again be filled with throngs of people going up to the House of the Lord with songs on their lips and joy in their hearts and a spotless lamb in tow. His heart was so full it must have almost exploded with the intensity of his desire for the nations of the world once again to acknowledge that Israel's Jehovah is God, and stand in awe of Him.

These thoughts must have been on Daniel's mind, because God answered in a very subtle yet symbolic way. Daniel clearly remembered, "While I was speaking and praying, confessing my sin and the sin of my people Israel and making my request to the LORD my God for his holy hill—while I was still in prayer, Gabriel, the man I had seen in the earlier vision, came to me in swift flight *about the time of the evening sacrifice*" (9:20–21, emphasis mine). That was an unmistakable message. God is not whimsical nor does He act randomly. He is very purposeful not only in what He says but in the way He says it and how He says it and when He says it.

So . . . why did God's answer to the Daniel Prayer come at the time of the evening sacrifice?

Think about it with me for a moment, because no one knows for sure. What we do know is that God answered Daniel's prayer immediately, while he was still praying. And we know God answered Daniel's prayer specifically, as we will see in the next chapter. Could it also be that God was focusing Daniel's attention on the ultimate answer?

Because the Daniel Prayer is a cry for freedom. It's a longing to go home. It's a full-court press, an all-consuming passion to see God's Name exalted, honored, respected, and revered as a result of His people being restored to the place of His blessing. Could it be that God was revealing a mystery? A secret? That the ultimate answer to all of the above would take place about five hundred years later? Around three o'clock in the afternoon, at the time of the evening sacrifice? On the Holy Hill of Calvary as the spotless Lamb of God was slain as a sacrifice for the sin of the world?

I want to be careful not to put words in God's mouth, but is it possible, in essence, that God was conveying something like the following?

Daniel, I've heard and will answer your prayer. I will set your people free. They will go home. Jerusalem and the temple will be rebuilt. Sacrifices will take place once again. But beloved, highly esteemed Daniel, there is more. Much more. The city of Jerusalem and the temple there are just replicas. They are shadows of a Heavenly Home where one day I will dwell with My people forever.[3] And the sacrifices are just audio-visual aids that point to My Lamb. Every time someone sacrifices in the temple, I have given them an invisible IOU note. Because the blood of lambs, bulls, and goats can never take away sin.[4] So one day, I will send My own Son as the Lamb who will die for the sin of the world.[5] His death will pay up in full all of those IOU notes. And forever after, anyone and everyone who places their faith in Him will be forgiven of their sin, cleansed of their guilt, and saved from My judgment. One day, Daniel, they will truly be free at last! Free once and for all from sin's penalty and sin's power. One day My Son will open the gates of Heaven and all those who trust in Him will live forever with Me in the New Jerusalem.[6] One day they will all go Home! O Daniel, there is an ultimate answer to your prayer, and His Name is Jesus!

I am convinced that the ultimate answer to the Daniel Prayer today is still Jesus. Because people are still being held captive. They are not held captive necessarily by the Babylonians or the Persians, although some surely are, but they are being held by the real enemy of our souls, the devil. People today are as enslaved by the devil as surely as the people in Daniel's day were enslaved by the Babylonians. The devil has bound them in chains of sin and selfishness and lust and greed. The enslavement of men and women, old and young, of every nationality, language, and culture, is why I am compelled to pray that all people everywhere would be saved and come to a knowledge of the truth.[7]

And make no mistake about it. The truth is Jesus.[8] Jesus is the Liberator of our souls. He is the Terminator of our enemy. He is the Lamb of God who died to make atonement for our sin. But He is also the Lion of Judah who shouts a victory roar over anything and anyone, over everything and everyone, who would hold us in captivity. Jesus died to break our shackles of bondage to sin. He rose from the dead to open prison doors that we might enter into the real freedom of abundant, eternal life in His Name. He ascended to God's right hand of authority and power where even now He is praying, not the Daniel Prayer, but His own High Priestly Prayer over us.[9]

At this moment, He is working to build the New Jerusalem for us as a Heavenly Home where we will dwell with Him forever.[10] And one glorious day He will return to judge and rule the world. One day the nations of the world will become the Kingdom of our God and of His Christ! Hallelujah! "Hallelujah! Salvation and glory and power belong to our God,"[11] and to His Son, our Lord Jesus Christ. "Hallelujah! For our Lord God Almighty reigns. Let us rejoice and be glad and give him glory!"[12]

He is the Ultimate Answer. The Daniel Prayer moves Heaven and changes a nation as one person at a time fully embraces Jesus . . .

One person like the apostle Paul who testified, "Here is a trustworthy saying that deserves full acceptance: Christ Jesus came into the world to save sinners—of whom I am the worst. But for that very reason I was shown mercy so that in me, the worst of sinners, Christ Jesus might display his unlimited patience as an example for those who would believe on him and receive eternal life."[13] Paul went on to turn the entire world of his day upside down as he proclaimed the Ultimate Answer through his testimony, through his preaching, as well as through his writing, which comprises much of the New Testament.[14] In a little more than three hundred years after Paul, the Gospel had so permeated the known world that Christianity was adopted as the official religion of the Roman Empire. Paul had moved Heaven and changed the world.

One person like William Carey (1761–1834), a cobbler who heard God's call in the quietness of his shoe shop: "If it be the duty of all men to believe the Gospel . . . then it be the duty of those who are entrusted with the Gospel to endeavor to make it known among all nations." It is said that he burst into tears and responded with the words of Isaiah, "Here am I; send me."[15] He embraced the Ultimate Answer, and proclaimed the Gospel in India for forty-one years.

He is considered the greatest missionary of the modern world. He translated and published the Scriptures into forty differ-ent languages and successfully worked to ban *sati*, the practice of burning widows alive when their husbands died. One of his sermon titles that has been quoted thousands of times seems to summarize his life of service, "Expect great things from God.

Attempt great things for God." Heaven was moved and the nation of India was changed.[16]

One person like David Livingstone (1813–1873), who, at the age of ten, embraced Jesus as his Savior. Shortly thereafter, he stated his life's purpose, "It is my desire to show my attachment to the cause of Him who died for me by devoting my life to His service." His heart was broken by the thought that millions of people were dying without knowing the Gospel. He was specifically burdened for the African continent. And so he wrote, "As for me, I am determined to open up Africa or perish." His stated goal was for every African to have the opportunity to embrace Jesus. As a result, Heaven was moved and an entire continent was changed as David Livingstone's explorations and maps and message opened up the interior.

One person like Hudson Taylor (1832–1905). As a young man he forsook the faith of his parents but, at the age of seventeen, embraced Jesus as his personal Lord and Savior. As a British missionary, he founded the *China Inland Mission* to proclaim the Ultimate Answer for fifty-one years in every province of China. Heaven was moved and the nation was changed; today the Chinese church is one of the largest, fastest growing churches in the world as a result.

One person like C. T. Studd (1860–1931), the wealthy, privileged young man who became a nationally recognized expert cricket player and captain of his team at Eton College in England. At the age of eighteen, when he was confronted with the question, "Are you a Christian?" he wasn't convinced that he was. In his own words, he relates, "I got down on my knees and I did say 'thank you' to God. And right then and there joy and peace came into my soul. I knew then what it was to be 'born again,' and the

Bible which had been so dry to me before, became everything."
It is said that he was living proof of what it means to embrace
Jesus without counting the cost or without looking back. He
is remembered as saying, "Some wish to live within the sound
of Church or Chapel bell; I want to run a Rescue Shop within
a yard of hell." And so he did. Heaven was moved and nations
were changed as he went on to proclaim the Ultimate Answer to
China, India, and the heart of Africa.[17]

One person like Jim Elliot (1927–1956), who embraced Jesus
at the tender age of six. He was raised by parents who were
devoted to the Gospel and who encouraged him to be adventur-
ous as he lived for Christ. As a young adult, he felt called to share
the Ultimate Answer to the Quechua Indians of Ecuador. While
working with them, he heard of an unreached, violent group
whose name means "savage"—the Auca Indians. He and four
other missionaries made contact with the Aucas.

After receiving encouraging responses to their overtures,
the five missionaries landed their small plane along the Curaray
River, where they established a base. But in spite of the seeming
friendliness of the Indians they had encountered, all five young
men were speared to death. Even though Jim Elliot's life was
brief, it demonstrated his core belief as expressed in his most well-
known quote, "He is no fool who gives what he cannot keep to
gain that which he cannot lose."

Jim Elliot's powerful witness resounded around the world
when he was featured in a *Life* magazine cover story shortly after
his death. His wife, Elisabeth Elliot, a well-known author and
speaker herself, continued his legacy through writing two biographies that described his life and death, *Shadow of the Almighty* and
Through Gates of Splendor—biographies that expanded his ministry

by challenging a new generation to take the Gospel to the utter-
most parts of the earth. And in 2006 a movie was released, *End
of the Spear,* that chronicled the successful, continuing effort to
reach the natives of Ecuador. Heaven was moved and the Aucas,
as well as many "savages" in the civilized world, were radically,
eternally changed.

One man like Azzam, a former pirate somewhere in Somalia
today, who rides in coffins, under corpses, because he knows
Somali Muslims will not open a casket or touch a dead body,
much less look under it. So Azzam "safely" rides in caskets
underneath corpses, traveling outside of Somalia where he then
is given a load of Bibles in Kenya. He travels back into Somalia
in a coffin, under a corpse, with the precious cargo of God's
Word that many people in his area are desperate to read. How
could he have ever come to the decision to engage in such a
mission?

Azzam had been born and raised a Muslim but had been
having dreams of Jesus. He had sought out his Imam for
answers, but the man had violently berated and beaten him.
When his mother discovered he was having Jesus dreams, she
commanded him to leave the home for his own protection and
never come back. He did. He walked miles and miles, quite sure
his father would be unable to find him.

But he was wrong. His father was a powerful warlord who
located him quickly, and sent Azzam a package. When Azzam
opened it, he was shocked and sickened to find his mother, cut
up into small pieces. A photograph had been included inside the
plastic bag. It was a picture of his mother kneeling in front of
two men who had their knives raised over her. The day Azzam
opened the "package" is the day he embraced the Ultimate

Answer as he committed his life to Jesus Christ as his Lord and Savior.

This is where the story gets even more incredible. Because Azzam sought out the two men who had butchered his mother. He told them that he forgave them. He told them that Jesus loved them and that He could forgive murderers. The two men, Mahdi and Yasin, embraced the Ultimate Answer and claimed Jesus as their Savior. Then they confided to Azzam, "As we killed your mother, her last words were, 'Jesus, Jesus, I love You.'"

Without a doubt, Heaven has been and is being moved by these radical followers of Jesus. And while Somalia has yet to be changed, it will be. One heart at a time.[18]

Because the Ultimate Answer to the Daniel Prayer . . . the Ultimate Answer that moves Heaven and changes a nation is not politics . . .

Or education.

Or a strong military.

Or nuclear weapons.

Or religion.

Or a particular denomination.

Or better organization.

Or capitalism.

Or socialism.

Or radicalism.

Or more jobs.

Or more money.

The Ultimate Answer is Jesus!

So don't just pray the Daniel Prayer. Become part of the Ultimate Answer to it by embracing Jesus fully. Then give Him to someone else by sharing the Gospel. Heaven will be moved. Our nation and world will be changed. One person at a time. *For the glory of His Name!*

Gideon was a man who lived in Israel before the time of kings when the nation was guided by judges. He was a timid man, who, in his own words, was a member of the weakest tribe in Israel, as well as the least member of his family. He was so afraid of the invading Midianites and the ravaging destruction they left in their wake that he threshed his wheat under the cover of the winepress.

One day his work was observed by a Man who sat down under a nearby oak tree. Just watching. Then the Man remarked to this timid farmer, "The Lord is with you, mighty warrior." I expect Gideon looked around to see who the Man was speaking to because surely no one would address him in that way. But the Man was speaking to Gideon. The Man was the Lord.

The Lord told Gideon He had chosen him to deliver Israel from the Midianites. That was not only astounding, I find it encouraging. God saw Gideon's potential—and yours and mine—when no one else sees it, including ourselves. God knew that if Gideon depended on Him alone and went forth in His power, he would indeed be a mighty, victorious warrior.

Gideon thought this would be a good time to pray. Specifically. I don't think the way that Gideon prayed indicated he lacked faith. Instead, he obviously needed assurance from God that he had accurately understood what to him must have been a shocking assignment. Which is very legitimate when obedience to what he understood would require not only risking his own life, but the lives of many others as well as putting his entire nation in a vulnerable position. So Gideon prayed specifically by laying out a fleece. Literally. He told God, "If you will save Israel by my hand as you have promised—look, I will place a wool fleece on the threshing floor. If there is dew only on the fleece and all the ground is dry, then I will know" . . . And that is what happened. Gideon rose early the next day; he squeezed the fleece and wrung out the dew, which filled a bowl with water.

Still needing reassurance of what to him must have been an unbelievable commission, he put out a second fleece, only, "This time make the fleece dry and the ground covered with dew." The next morning when Gideon checked, the fleece was dry and the ground all around it was wet. So Gideon knew he had rightly understood the Word of the Lord. He went out in God's supernatural power and defeated the Midianites.[1]

While I have not made a habit of putting out a fleece, and don't encourage others to do so, Gideon's example reminds us to be specific in our prayer requests. Do you pray specifically? It's been said that the person who asks God for nothing won't be disappointed. In other words, people are afraid if they pray specifically they will be setting themselves up for disappointment when God doesn't answer specifically.

I know parents who don't teach their children to pray specifically because they are so afraid their children's faith will be damaged when God doesn't answer specifically. Their cautious attitude, of course, does its own damage to their children's faith by teaching them that He doesn't answer specific prayer.

People who don't pray specifically may not be disappointed but they surely miss out on the thrill of moving Heaven as evidenced by the specific answers God does give. God may still bless them and give them an answer. It's just that they won't recognize it as the answer because they never specified what they were asking of Him. I know what it's like to pray generally and miss out on the blessing of receiving a specific answer. But I also know what it's like to pray specifically.

God has answered many specific prayers for me, from small requests such as . . .

> Locating an empty handicapped parking place when I took my husband to his doctor,
>
> Finding the right gift for someone's birthday,
>
> Bringing the dog back when he's run out of the yard,
>
> Helping my granddaughter pull up her math grade,
>
> Locating my husband's misplaced hearing aid—for the hundredth time,
>
> Ensuring that the apple pie I make for Daddy is the best ever.

To larger requests such as . . .

> Inspiring thoughts, and the words to express them, for this book,
>
> Meeting the deadline for submitting the manuscript,
>
> Breaking open a passage of Scripture so that I have the framework for a message,
>
> Opening my mind to understand the Scripture and how it applies to my life and the lives of those in my audience,

Giving me wisdom to answer media questions so that
people are drawn to Jesus,

Timing my message on a tight platform program so that I
don't rob time from the person who follows me,

Releasing my husband from the hospital in time for
Christmas Day at home,

Enabling me to remain alert as I stayed with my Mother all
night before she moved to Our Father's House.

To much greater requests such as . . .

Quickening someone's heart to embrace Jesus as Savior
and Lord,

Healing my husband of the MRSA infection in his dialysis
fistula,

Freeing me from anger and bitterness as I chose to forgive
those who wounded me,

Expanding my opportunities to give out God's Word while
I stayed at home to care for my husband,

Bringing just the right people—my "generals"—to come
alongside me and work at my ministry office . . .

Previously I shared with you about the immediate answer to
prayer God had given me through His messenger, Ray Bentley,
the husband of one of my board members. When three of my
ministry directors left, this dear man had told me simply and
plainly, "Anne, God will bring you generals." If I remember cor-
rectly, I think I muttered something like, "I hope He brings them
quickly." I knew not only my staff, but the ministry initiatives I
was responsible for, were hanging in the balance, and time was
passing.

On the Monday morning after I returned home from the meeting where I had been encouraged by the promise of generals, I joined my staff for prayer. I had made it a habit of joining with them every Monday morning, so that we start our week together in worship and praise, focusing on the One who has called us and who equips us to serve Him. I shared with those gathered how I had been encouraged by God's messenger. Then I asked them to pray with me for the Generals. We all prayed. Intensely. Humbly. Sincerely. Specifically we asked God to bring to us additional personnel for each area that was lacking. And we asked Him to bring the Generals to us. I, for one, did not want to have to go through public advertising, postings on church bulletin boards, or even lengthy interview procedures that would take up time I didn't feel we could spare.

One by one, over the space of the next six months, God brought us His choice for the staff positions. To be honest, it was a little slower than I would have liked. I know now, and I knew even then, that God was testing my faith by stretching things out. It was a thrilling adventure—a roller-coaster ride of extreme ups and downs.

The first General God brought to us was something of a surprise, because he was a "he." Up until this point in our office, we had been staffed by women. But God was doing a new thing. He brought us a great big guy nicknamed "Blindside" who not only helped with the logistics of our events, but whose humble spirit and sense of humor breathed the fresh air of the Spirit into our midst. The next was a single woman who helped coordinate our events. And then came a most remarkable young mother, who has an engineering degree and easily took over our IT issues and website.

God brought me a director for our revivals who was the very best I could have imagined—smart, hardworking, capable, experienced, who loved me and loved the ministry. While I rejoiced over each person God brought on staff, I knew the most important position of all had yet to be filled. It was the position of Operations Manager. I knew we needed someone who could oversee all the bits and pieces of the ministry while keeping everything on track and everyone working well together. And so I prayed. And prayed. And fasted. And prayed some more.

As names were submitted for my attention and resumes forwarded for this position, I interviewed at least four people with the help of board members. We all agreed none of them seemed to be the general we were looking for. And then a résumé came to me in one of those "by the way" encounters that seemed so casual as to be irrelevant. But when I read through the résumé, something seemed to click. I heard the still, small voice of the Spirit whispering, "This is the one." Once again, I was more than intrigued because it was a man.

I set up a time to meet with this man one-on-one and go through the now familiar questions of the interview. Because this position would affect our entire office, and because this person would interact not only with every staff person, but with the board and me, I felt I could not risk making a mistake. So I did something I almost never do. I laid out a "fleece." I did not lack faith. Instead, I was seeking clear confirmation for God's perfect will in the course of action I would take because it involved the well-being of so many other people, and the well-being of my ministry as a whole.

Like Gideon, putting out a fleece is, in a sense, asking God for a sign. It's asking God to confirm a decision or course of action with a specific answer. A fleece should be something that's logical but not probable unless God intervenes and brings it to pass, thus confirming a course of action or decision. As I was praying before the first interview, I asked God to give me His idea for a fleece. The thought that came to my mind was this: I asked God to have the gentleman ask me what name he should call me.

In all the interviews I've conducted in the thirty years AnGeL Ministries has been in existence, no one has ever asked me what they should call me. Because the staff had always been made up of women, it seemed natural that I had always been called by my first name. But with a man I thought it might be different. So it wasn't probable that this person would ask me what he should call me, but it still seemed within the realm of reason.

When the time came for the interview, I saw an unfamiliar car pull into the parking lot. Assuming it was the prospective operations manager, I went to the door of the office to greet him and put him at ease. We shook hands warmly, then as I guided him into the lobby area, he looked over his shoulder and said, "What should I call you?"[2] I almost fell over! I had to restrain myself from shouting, "You're hired!" I will tell you that rather than an interview, I actually gave a very intense sales pitch.

The man left that day feeling positive, while I was ecstatic. But we had two more rounds of interviews to go. One of my board members called him to go over practical details that included salary and benefits. When she reported to me what she had told him, I realized that she had told him one salary figure and I had told him another one.

So as I went into the second one-on-one interview with him, I decided to put out another fleece. I asked God, when the question of his salary came up, to have him tell me the figure didn't matter. I knew that was highly improbable for a man who was married with two college-age sons. But I was so afraid of making a mistake, and I was so desperate for God's perfect choice, and I was so aware that I could react emotionally to the relief of possibly having found someone for this position that I would jump ahead of the Lord, that I just had to be sure.

As we met for the second interview, the subject of his salary came up. I told him that I had stated one figure and my board member had stated another. While I apologized for the confusion, I asked him for his thoughts. He responded by saying, "Miss Anne, it doesn't make any difference. Whatever you offer is fine." My second fleece was answered!

The third test I put this patient gentleman through was for him to sit down with all the staff and allow them to interview him. Their questions were specific, some were tough, some were personal, all were used of God to penetrate below the surface and reveal the type of person he is. When he shared the testimony of his conversion, he wept. And we all wept with him as our hearts embraced the humble servant-leader God had brought to us as our last general. And we all hired him.

If I hadn't known it before, I knew it then with certainty. God answers specific prayers specifically. Don't miss out on the thrill of discovering that your prayers have moved Heaven because you pray generally. Pray specifically. Who knows how God has already been at work? When we ask God for what He wants to give us, we can be fairly sure He has a plan already in place. Our specific prayer gives us the thrill of not only participating in what He is doing, but knowing that we are part of a Divine plan.

One hundred years before the Daniel Prayer was prayed, God had put in place a plan that was revealed by Isaiah the prophet . . . "This is what the LORD says . . . who says of Cyrus, 'He is my shepherd and will accomplish all that I please; he will say of Jerusalem, 'Let it be rebuilt,' and of the temple, 'Let its foundations be laid.'"[3]

Keep in mind that Isaiah wrote this prophecy before the Babylonians invaded. Before the Jews were led off into captivity. Before Jerusalem was destroyed. Before the temple was looted and leveled. And if that wasn't dramatic enough, God had given to Isaiah one hundred years earlier further insight when He revealed,

> This is what the LORD says to his anointed, to Cyrus, whose right hand I take hold of to subdue nations before him . . . to open doors before him . . . I will go before you . . . I will give you the treasures . . . so that you may know that I am the LORD, the God of Israel, who summons you by name. For the sake of . . . Israel my chosen, I summon you by name and bestow on you a title of honor, though you do not acknowledge me. I am the LORD, and there is no other; apart from me there is no God. I will strengthen you . . . so that from the rising of the sun to the place of its setting men may know there is none besides me. I am the LORD, and there is no other.[4]

In other words, God would do all of this using Cyrus for the glory of His Name!

When Daniel prayed his urgent plea, he was asking God to do for him what God had already not only promised to do, but according to a plan that God had already put in motion. While we know that Daniel knew of God's promise through Jeremiah, we are not told if Daniel knew of God's plan spoken through

Isaiah. But he didn't need to know God's plan any more than you or I need to know God's plan. That's where our faith takes over.

God's promises are enough on which to base our prayers. We don't necessarily need to see the big picture or the grander scheme of things to move Heaven and change nations. Our prayer is to be centered on God, not on a plan that we are trying to figure out or help Him accomplish.

In essence, Daniel was pleading,

> O God, please. Deliver us from our enemies. Restore us to the place of Your blessing. We humbly, sincerely acknowledge we have sinned. We are so sorry. What else can we say? What else can we do? We know we deserve to be in captivity, so we throw ourselves on Your great mercy. Forgive us for our sin. We bow in confidence before You because You are faithful. You promised through Jeremiah that after seventy years You would release us from our captors and we believe that You are a God of Your word. I've been in captivity for sixty-seven years. So God, please, in three years release us from Your judgment! Let us go home! Bring life back to Jerusalem. Fulfill Your promise. Set us free. Revive us! For the glory of Your Name.

Heaven was moved in a dramatic, specific way. God kept His promise and He answered Daniel's prayer. Specifically. Supernaturally.

Three years later, a new king took the throne in Persia. His name? Cyrus! And what was one of his first proclamations as the new king? It was a proclamation that he issued verbally but also made sure it was in writing so that all could hear and read what he said, including you and me over 2,500 years later. This was his proclamation . . .

The LORD, the God of heaven, has given me all the kingdoms of the earth and he has appointed me to build a temple for him at Jerusalem in Judah. Anyone of his people among you—may his God be with him, and let him go up to Jerusalem in Judah and build the temple of the LORD, the God of Israel, the God who is in Jerusalem.[5]

There was no reason for the heart of Cyrus to be moved to let all God's people go home except that Daniel had prayed . . . and God had answered!

Even more phenomenal is that Cyrus was quoting Isaiah's prophecy when he declared God had appointed him to build a temple for Him in Jerusalem. Did he have a copy of the Scriptures? Had someone read it to him? How had he come to know what God had prophesied concerning his reign one hundred years earlier? It's incredible the way all the details fit together like pieces in a jigsaw puzzle, revealing the glory of a great God who hears and answers prayer!

Not only did Cyrus tell all the Jews who wanted to leave that they could go home, but he gave them building materials for the temple. He gave them money. And he restored the temple vessels of gold and silver that had been looted by Nebuchadnezzar seventy years earlier.[6]

So . . . three years after Daniel prayed and seventy years after their captivity had begun, a remnant of God's people under the leadership of Zerubbabel and Jeshua began their long eight-hundred-mile journey from Persia back home. Did they run the entire distance with the joy of knowing they were going home? Did they sing around the campfire every night the Psalms of Ascent as they looked forward to going up to the House of the Lord once again? Did they laugh and excitedly share their hopes and dreams with each other as the pain of their past captivity was momentarily forgotten in the new flush of anticipation?

Then they arrived. And reality set in.

What must it have been like to climb up the last of the Judean hills and look on the pile of rubble that had been the City of David? The city of Jerusalem? The city of their God? How did they feel as they wandered through the burned out houses and the broken-down buildings? Did tears flow freely as they picked their way through the ruins of what had been the temple? Did they almost whisper to each other, "Look! That's where the altar used to be. And that's where the Holy Place was. And that's where the Most Holy Place . . ."

Did their words choke on their emotions as they saw everything they remembered was no more? Did they sit for a while in a dumbfounded silence broken only by quiet sobbing as each one gazed on what appeared to be their nightmare in 3D? Who was the first one to get up and say, "Enough already. We didn't travel eight hundred miles to sit around and cry like babies. Let's get to work."

So they did. To the eternal credit of the remnant's courage and strength of resolve, inspired by the prophets Haggai and Zechariah,[7] they went to work, cleared the stones, and rebuilt the temple. When their initial work was completed and the temple was finished, the sound of weeping could be heard again. The old men were crying because to them the rebuilt temple seemed "like nothing" compared to the glory of Solomon's original temple that they remembered.

God heard their cries and encouraged them by promising that He would "fill this house with glory . . . the glory of this present house will be greater than the glory of the former house."[8] Once again, God was true to His word. Although the remnant had no way of knowing at the time, the house of God they rebuilt and King Herod later remodeled was the very place in which the baby Jesus was presented to God.[9]

Twelve years after his presentation in the temple, it was the same place that the young boy Jesus sat "among the teachers, listening to them and asking them questions," amazing everyone with His understanding and His answers.[10] Although He returned to His home in the Galilean region for another eighteen years, when He began His public ministry, Jesus of Nazareth, the Lamb of God, the Messiah, the Redeemer of Israel, the Son of God and the Son of Man, returned to walk in the same temple courts, to sit and teach on the same temple steps. And His presence "filled this house with glory."

I wonder . . . when the remnant who had returned from Persia offered the first sacrifice in the newly rebuilt temple, and the first tendril of smoke rose above the pinnacle like a gray banner against the cobalt-blue sky beckoning God's people to worship Him once again on His Holy Hill, did they ever know that Daniel had prayed? I think not.

They didn't see in the shadows eight hundred miles east the figure of an old man with a long gray beard. A man who was so old that he was too old to make the trip to Jerusalem. A man unable to fulfill his life's dream of seeing Jerusalem once again. An old man looking out his open window with ashes smeared on his face, dressed in sackcloth, fasting, praying, pleading, pouring out his heart as he stood in the gap for his people. Holding God to His word as he prayed specifically.

What difference does the prayer of one person make? You will never know until you pray. So . . . pray! *Now!*

PART FOUR

PATTERNS
FOR PRAYER

The prayer of the upright
pleases him.

PROVERBS 15:8

Because my husband's health was in
decline, I had cut back on my traveling and speaking so that I
could stay home and care for him. As a result, I had time to be
quiet and listen more to the whispers of the Spirit. He revealed
things to me in the stillness that I'm not sure I would have heard
in my prior chaotic busyness.

Looking back over this time when I was closer to home, I am
intrigued to recognize that God intentionally placed me there
to focus more on prayer and assigned me the privilege of calling
others to prayer. As of this writing, five different times God has
deeply burdened me to offer online prayer initiatives. Each one
has been distinctly different. Each one drew tens of thousands
of participants. And for each one I wrote prayers that I sent out
by email on a daily basis during the initiative.[1] My purpose was
not just to ask people to pray, but to lead them in prayer so that
we would all be on the same page as we prayed. God poured out
His blessing on these initiatives, and we have seen many, many
answers to our prayers.

The response I received to these initiatives helped me grasp
the fact that many people want to pray, but like me, they just
need some help and direction in their prayers. Therefore, because
I have challenged you in the pages of this book to pray the Daniel

Prayer, I wondered if you might also be more inclined to do so if I led you in it.

On the following pages I have written a prayer for each of the sections that I outlined in Daniel's prayer. These prayers are not meant to be ritualistic or formalized. They are simply offered as patterns for your own prayers.[2]

A PRAYER THAT IS CENTERED

After this I looked, and there before me was a door standing open in heaven. . . . At once I was in the Spirit, and there before me was a throne in heaven with someone sitting on it.

REVELATION 4:1–2

Enthroned Living Lord . . .

Everything revolves around You. Everything. We worship You as . . .

the Center-point of the Universe,

the Center-point of time and space,

the Center-point of history,

the Center-point of life, meaning, and purpose today,

the Center-point of all of our tomorrows,

the Center-point of prayer.

You are the Center-point. Period.

Nothing really matters except Your will and Your wants and Your way and Your Word.

How could we have become so out of focus? Our distorted perspective is rooted in our hearts, twisted in our minds, then reflected in our prayers. Because . . .

What we have wanted seems so vital,

What we have thought seems so critical,
What we have felt seems so crucial,
What we have said sounds so spiritual,
We seem to be consumed with ourselves!
We ourselves seem to be the center-point as we pray. We are so ashamed. In the light of who You are, we now get it. We understand that it's what You want that is vital, what You think that is so critical, what You feel that is crucial, what You say is the wisdom of the ages expressed in unvarnished, eternal truth. How could we have set ourselves up as gods, and expected You to fall in line with us? We're so sorry for spending the majority of our prayers thanking You for what You have done for us, and asking You to do something else for us, as though You exist for our personal benefit.

We choose now to make You the Center-point of our lives and of our prayers. We want what You want more than what we want. What You think matters more to us than what anyone else thinks, including ourselves. We want to feel Your heart and speak Your word to a world that desperately needs a Center-point.

Now, in the privacy of this place, with utmost sincerity, necessity, and humility, we plead with You for what You have purposed to give, for what You have wanted to do, for what You have promised to fulfill in Your Word. We want Your kingdom to come, Your will to be done on earth as it is in Heaven. We want to be a part of what You are doing . . . to come alongside You as You accomplish Your perfect plan.

We believe You will hear and answer us because . . .

. . . We come to You in the name of Your "Son, whom [You have] appointed heir of all things."[1]

. . . We come to You in the name of the One by whom "all things were created: things in heaven and on earth, visible and invisible, whether thrones or powers or rulers or authorities; all things were created by him and for him. He is before all things, and in him all things hold together."[2]

. . . We come to You in the name of the One who is the radiance of Your glory, the exact representation of Your being.[3]

. . . We come to You in the name of the One who sustains all things by His powerful word.[4]

. . . We come to You in the name of the Creator who became our Savior and who has ascended into Heaven to sit at Your right hand, with all authority placed under His feet.[5]

. . . We come to You humbly, yet boldly, because we have been invited to come.[6]

. . . We come to You with confidence because the way has been opened for us by the blood of Your Son who sits at Your right hand, who is in authority over all.[7]

. . . We come to You with a sincere heart in full assurance of faith that You will receive us, You will listen to us, and You will answer us.[8]

Because we come to You in the name of JESUS.

For the glory of Your Name.

Amen.

A PRAYER THAT IS COMPELLED

His word is in my heart like a fire, a
fire shut up in my bones. I am weary
of holding it in; indeed, I cannot.

JEREMIAH 20:9

Our Father, who is in Heaven, we worship You as the
living God of Daniel. You set the heavens in place and
laid the foundations of the earth.[1] In a world that changes
and undulates like the surface of the sea, You and Your
Word are unshaken. You are the Creator who spoke
everything into existence through the power of Your
Word.[2] Your thoughts are as high above our thoughts
as the heavens are higher than the earth.[3] Who could
know what's on Your mind and in Your heart except as
You choose to reveal Yourself to us? And You have! You
are Light.[4] You have made Yourself visible and knowable
through the pages of our Bibles. And Your Word is our
life.[5] It is eternal; it stands firm in the heavens.[6] There is
no shadow of turning with You.[7] From age to age, from
generation to generation, You and Your Word do not
change.

Thank You for being utterly trustworthy. We find security and hope in knowing we can take You at Your Word. You are a Gentleman. You do not mock Your children. We can stand firmly on Your promises, which are like prophecy. They will come to pass because what You say is so. They resonate deep within our hearts; like sparks of life falling on our dry spirits, they ignite a holy passion for You and what You want.

When we lack fire and zeal for You, Your Word, Your will and Your wants, we have only to look at the priority we have given to our Bible reading and study. We confess we have been neglectful of Your Word. There are days when we go without reading it. And there are many days when we read it but we don't take the time to process what we are reading. When we close our Bibles we don't even remember what we read. No wonder we don't know how to pray! So when we do pray we have cared more about our wants than Your wants. We often tell You what's on our minds without ever asking what's on Yours. We pour out our hearts to You, but quickly leave our prayer time without waiting to listen to Your heart. We have been . . .

deaf to Your voice,

willful in our ways,

self-centered in our wants,

shallow in our thoughts,

and miserly in our love.

We are deeply ashamed.

Let us know that the work of prayer is to bring our wills to Yours,

And that without this it is folly to pray;
When we try to bring Your will to ours it is to
command You,
    to be above You,
    and wiser than You;
this is our sin and pride.
We can only succeed when we pray
    According to Your precept and promise,
    According to Your sovereign will.

And now, O God who has ears to hear and listens to Your children as we pray, we ask that You would teach us to pray according to Your Word. We want our wills to conform to Yours. Mold our lives according to Your Word. We want to ask You for what You have already purposed to give us, to do for us, and to do through us, yet will not do so until we ask. We don't want to get to Heaven and discover all the answers to prayer for which we never bothered to ask You, because we were ignorant of Your Word.[8] We don't want to get to Heaven and hear of all the blessings You wanted to pour out on others through us, only to find that our self-focus and self-centeredness had blocked the flow.

So come down, most Holy Lord. Look on our world . . .
    On the battlefields and the mine fields,
    On the corruption and the destruction,
    On the greed and the need,
    On the strategy sessions and the spinning deception,
    On the sin that's flaunted and the sin that's hidden,
    On the murders and the misery,

On the abuse and the arrogance,

On the victim and the vice . . .

On our foundation that is cracking,

On our nation that is crumbling,

On Your church that is sleeping,

On Your people who are crying out to You.

Teach us to pray according to Your Word with such power that Heaven is moved and our nation, and our world, are changed.

We ask all of these things in the name of the One who said, "Here I am . . . I have come to do your will, O God . . ."[9] then got up from Heaven's throne, made Himself nothing, took on the very nature of a servant, being made in human likeness. And being found in appearance as a man, he humbled Himself and became obedient to death—even death on a cross![10]

We pray in the name of the One whom You have exalted to the highest place . . . the One to whom You have given the name that is above every name . . .[11]

We pray in the name of JESUS.

For the glory of Your Name.

Amen.

A PRAYER THAT IS CONFIDENT

"Did I not tell you that if you believed, you would see the glory of God?"

JOHN 11:40

Great God of Creation, Lord of the Universe, the God who parted the Red Sea, You are the God of the impossible who makes a way when there is no way. We worship You as our God. We exalt You as One whose Name is above every name. You have no equal. You stand in the solitude of Yourself.

Your righteous right hand hung the stars in space, shattered Your enemies, and holds us, Your children by covenant, safe and secure.[1] Who is like You—majestic in holiness, awesome in glory, working wonders?[2]

By Your word everything was made that is in heaven or on earth or under the earth.[3] You formed us from the dust of the ground, breathed Your breath into us, and gave us life.[4] When we disobeyed, rebelled against You, and lived in bondage to sin, You sent the Deliverer to give His life to set us free. By Your great power, You raised Him from the dead so that through faith in Him we are rescued from the dominion of darkness and brought into the kingdom of Your light and life and love.[5]

We worship You as One who maintains Your faithfulness to all generations.[6] Just as You were faithful to Abraham, Isaac, and Jacob; to Moses, Jeremiah, and Daniel; to Peter, Paul, and John; You will be faithful to us and to our children and to our grandchildren. You can't be less than Yourself, and You are faithful. You keep Your "covenant of love to a thousand generations of those who love [You] and keep [Your] commandments."[7]

And we praise You as One who is never wrong. You are always right. As we witness unspeakable disasters, atrocities and evil, we are confident that the Judge of all the earth does right. And will do right.[8] All the time.

We know Your timing is perfect. If we see no outward evidence that You are intervening in the affairs of men, we trust You. If we see no sparks of revival in the church, we trust You. If we see no cessation in hostilities and persecutions against those who are called by Your Name, we trust You. If we do not receive an answer to our prayers when we want it, the way we want it, how we want it, we trust You.

We are confident that Your greatness and power are the same yesterday in Creation, in the Exodus, in Daniel's day, as it is in our day, as it will be at the end of time. Your greatness has not been diluted or depleted over the ages. You cannot be more great than You are. You are the All-Mighty God. And we worship You.

Thank You, loving Lord, for being a covenant-making, covenant-keeping God. Thank You that through the broken body and shed blood of Your Son and our Savior, the Lord Jesus Christ, we can enter into a covenant with You that will never be broken. Thank You that we are Yours, and You are ours . . . forever. Thank You for the confidence that our covenant relationship with You gives us as we approach You in prayer.

You have said that You are holy, high and lifted up, but that You are moved to come down—to dwell—with those who are contrite and lowly in spirit.[9] We believe You! You have said that You will revive the heart of the contrite.[10] We believe You! You have said that if we repent of our sin, times of refreshing will come. We believe You![11]

So now we want to honestly confess that in our previous prayers we have not been focused on You. We have focused on our circumstances and have therefore been defeated. We have focused on others and have therefore been deluded. We have focused on ourselves and have therefore been deceived. We compare ourselves with others so that our perception of who we really are therefore is distorted. We are so sorry. We turn to You now and ask that You shine the light of Your truth into our hearts and what we feel and into our minds and what we think so that we see ourselves as You see us, and truly repent of our sin.

Strip us, most Holy Lord, of any pride or self-righteousness or judgment as we pray for others. Teach us to first take the plank out of our own eye before trying to remove the splinter in someone else's eye.[12] We long for You to send revival to the hearts of Your people. Let it begin with us. Teach us to pray in such a way that Heaven is moved and hearts are changed.

We pray in the name of the One who was so confident in Your Word that when facing the threats of His accusers, He issued a solemn warning that in the future, their roles would be reversed. He would be their Judge. They would see Him sitting at Your right hand and coming back on the clouds of glory . . .[13]

We pray in the name of the One who was so confident in You that He placed His very life in Your hands, and then refused to draw the next breath.[14]

We pray in the name of JESUS.

For the glory of Your Name.

Amen.

A PRAYER THAT IS CONTRITE

Return . . . to the LORD your God.
Your sins have been your downfall!
Take words with you, and return to the LORD.
Say to him: "Forgive all our sins."

HOSEA 14:1–2

God of grace and God of glory . . .

You are righteous and holy and pure. You are the Light of the world.[1] In You is no darkness at all.[2] No shadow of turning.

Please, Most Holy Lord, Most Merciful Savior, hear us as we pray with contrition.

CONTRITE FOR PERSONAL SIN AND SHAME

You have "clothed me with garments of salvation and arrayed me in a robe of [Your] righteousness . . . as a bride adorns herself with her jewels,"[3]

But in my Christian walk I am still in rags;
My best prayers are stained with sin;
My penitential tears are muddied with self.

I need to repent of my repentance;

I need my tears to be washed . . .

I have sinned times without number,

And been guilty of pride and unbelief,

Of failure to find thy mind in thy Word,

Of neglect to seek thee in my daily life. *

Now I earnestly plead with You, Divine Gardener of my heart,

Break up the fallow ground . . .

I confess that I have run from Your marvelous light back into dark areas of old habits, forbidden relationships, and seductive pleasures.

I repent.

I confess I have given You leftover money, leftover time, and even leftover love, implying You are second-best.

I repent.

I confess that I have cared more about what my neighbor says, than what You say; of being more afraid of what my employer or government official thinks, than what You think; of being so intimidated by the opinions of others that I have been silent and do not boldly proclaim who You are.

I repent.

I confess that I have cared more about my own reputation than Yours so that while I give You the glory, I take a 10 percent commission and so diminish Your Name.

I repent.

I confess that my priorities, actions, and decisions reveal I have honored and exalted myself, my friends, my family, other people, and even my wallet, above You.

I repent.

I confess that I have closed my eyes and ears to the needs of others around me because I want more for myself.

I repent.

I confess that I have looked to the president or to a pastor or to a priest or to a government agency for the help I need before I look to You.

I repent.

I confess that I have honored You with my lips, while my heart has been far from You.

I repent.

I confess . . .

I am so slow to learn,
So prone to forget
So weak to climb;
I am in the foothills when I should be on the heights;
I am pained by my graceless heart,
My prayerless days,
My poverty of love,
My sloth in the heavenly race,
My sullied conscience,
My wasted hours,
My unspent opportunities,
I am blind while light shines around me:
Take the scales from my eyes,
Grind to dust the evil heart of unbelief.
Destroy in me every lofty thought,
Break pride to pieces and scatter it to the winds,
Annihilate each clinging shred of self-righteousness,
Implant in me true lowliness of spirit . . .
Open in me a fount of penitential tears,
Break me, then bind me up . . .

CONTRITE FOR SIN WITHIN THE CHURCH

We confess that as a church, Your Body, we have often placed a higher priority on programs than on prayer, on activities than on the Spirit's life, on orthodoxy than on obedience, on religious rituals than on a personal relationship with You.

We confess we have done our work without Your power.

We confess that we label each other as liberal or conservative, moderate or fundamentalist, progressive or charismatic, traditional or contemporary, and so we do not "make every effort to keep the unity of the Spirit through the bond of peace."[4]

We confess that we don't really know what we believe, or why we should believe, and are therefore too weak to stand against the assault of the enemy or to resist the erosion of doctrine.

We confess that we have been ashamed of the Gospel as we have not declared it boldly to this generation for fear of offending someone of another religion.

We confess to our racial prejudice that draws boundary lines in worship between "us" and "them."

We confess to spending more money on our buildings than on our ministries and missions.

We confess to adapting Your Truth to the politically correct culture of our day, so that Your Light is dimmed.

We confess to caring more about church growth than being "salt" and "light."

We confess that we have hidden Your glory in our denominational loyalty that leads to divisiveness and exclusiveness so that we make others feel they are on the periphery of Your inner circle, and thus feel alienated from You.

We confess that we have excluded and wounded those who have wounded us, or who are not like us, or who do not measure up to our standards, so that our fellowship is not a safe place as the cycle of pain is perpetuated within Your Body, diminishing the radiance of Your unconditional love, mercy, and grace.

We confess that we have offered the world a tarnished reflection of You by our own bitterness, meanness, unforgiveness, pridefulness, unkindness, rudeness, self-righteousness, and other sins so that we have made people think less of You.

We confess that we have given others the impression that You tolerate sin because we do.

Lamb of God . . .

Your blood is like a great river of infinite grace
    With never any diminishing of its fullness
    As thirsty ones without number drink of it.
The Cross is not just for "them." It's for us.
Wash us clean in the ocean of Your blood.
Prepare Your Church to be a spotless, holy, beautiful Bride for our Bridegroom when He comes to receive us to Himself.

CONTRITE FOR NATIONAL SIN AND SHAME

We confess we no longer fear You, and thus we have not even the beginning of wisdom with which to handle the vast knowledge we possess.

We confess our foolishness of denying You as the one, true, living God, our Creator to whom we are accountable, living as though our lives are a cosmic accident with no eternal significance, purpose or meaning.

We confess to our greed that has run up trillions of dollars of national debt.

We confess our arrogance and pride that has led us to think we are sufficient in ourselves.

We confess to believing that the prosperity of our nation is because we are great while refusing to acknowledge that all blessings come from Your hand.

We confess that we depend upon our military might and our weapons systems to protect us from harm and danger, while denying, defying, and ignoring You.

We confess that we have succumbed to the pressure of pluralism in our desire to be inclusive, so that we honor other gods as though You are just one of many.

We confess that we have allowed the material blessings You have given us to deceive us into thinking we don't need You.

We confess that we feel entitled to what someone else has earned, instead of taking responsibility for ourselves and our families as we trust You.

We confess that we live as though material wealth and prosperity will bring happiness.

We confess that we still judge a person's value, not by their character, but by the color of their skin.

We confess that we have promoted murder as our "right to choose," so that an entire generation of 57 million lives have been destroyed. Willfully. Intentionally.

We confess that we have accepted and even applauded that which You say is an abomination, while intimidating into silence those who uphold Your Word.

We confess that we have legalized defiance of Your design and plan for the family, as though the modern world no longer needs to live by the Creator's directions for life.

We confess that we have shown respect to Israel's enemies while resisting her right to the land You have given her.

We confess that we have become one nation under many gods, divided and polarized, with license to sin and justice that no longer follows the rule of law.

We confess that we have marginalized truth and mainstreamed lies.

Therefore . . . we reject pride and arrogance. We humble ourselves. We stop looking around and seek Your face. We rend our hearts! Please, let us stand in the gap for our nation.

With tears of shame, we come to You, Lamb of God . . .

We have confessed personal, corporate, and national sin.

Wash us clean. Bathe us in the cleansing fountain of blood that flows from Your pierced body. Then fill us with Your Holy Spirit. Now. We humbly, boldly ask.

Thank You for Your forgiveness.

Thank You for the Blood that washes us clean.

Thank You that our tears are on Your face.

Thank You that as our High Priest You understand firsthand the feelings of the shame and guilt of our sin.

Thank You that although You were sinless, You became sin for us that we might be right with You.

Thank You that when we are under Your blood and our lives are hidden in You, we become a new creation. . The old has gone, and the new has come.

Thank You for the blessed assurance that when we have confessed our sin—when we have been cleansed of our sin—we will receive a rich welcome into Your Presence and into Your Heavenly Home because our Savior is the only-begotten Son of the Father. We pray in His name, JESUS.

For the glory of Your Name

Amen.

A PRAYER THAT IS CLEAR

You do not have,
because
you do not ask God.

JAMES 4:2

Great God of Creation.
    God of Abraham, Isaac, and Jacob.
    Living God of Daniel.
    God and Father of our Lord Jesus Christ.
    We worship You alone.
    In the darkness, You are our Light.
    In the storm, You are our Anchor.
    In the face of terrorism, You are our Shield.
    In time of war, You are our Peace.
    In our weakness, You are our Strength.
    In our grief, You are our Comfort.
    In our despair, You are our Hope.
    In our confusion, You are our Wisdom.
    In times of uncertainty,
        when buildings implode,
            bombs explode,
                stock markets slide,

people commit suicide,

banks collapse,

businesses are bankrupted,

and homes are foreclosed . . .

When the nations rage and the people imagine a vain thing . . .

When the rulers take a stand and gather together against the Lord . . .[1]

When the earth beneath us breaks apart . . .

When the sky above us is torn by lightning and thunder . . .

When the air around us is a swirling dervish of violence . . .

When the mountains fall into the midst of the sea . . .

When the waters roar and foam . . .

When nations are in uproar and kingdoms fall . . .[2]

When everything gives way,

You are the Rock on which we stand![3]

Save us from ourselves.

Free us from the chokehold of sin.

Protect us from our enemies.

Spare us from Your judgment.

We are pleading with You for an outpouring of Your Spirit on us, on our families, on our churches, and on our nation. Send down Your Spirit in Pentecostal fullness! Captivate us by Your love! Rend our hearts with deep conviction and sorrow for our sin! Draw us back to the foot of the Cross. Plunge us beneath the fountain filled with His blood, then . . .

Revive our hearts!

Fill our hearts!

Ignite our hearts . . .

. . . with a pure and holy passion to love You and
to live our lives for You and for Your glory alone!

Then use us to bring revival to the hearts of Your
people!

We are asking You to saturate us in Your holiness,
purity, righteousness,

justice, power, mercy, grace, truth, and love.

Saturate us in Yourself, so that all may see You
reflected in us.

We are asking You to revive the confidence of our
faith and the authenticity of our personal relationship
with You.

We are asking for one more great spiritual awakening
before Jesus Christ returns to rapture the church and
bring judgment on the world.

O Holy God, look on Your people who are called by
Your Name. Hear our prayer. Listen to our pleas. Have
mercy on us. Let the Fire of the Holy Spirit fall fresh
on us!

You have promised that You will do whatever we
ask in Jesus' name.[4] So please, answer us. Answer us!
Answer us in JESUS' name.

For the glory of Your Name.

Amen.

I pray also that the eyes of your heart may be enlightened in order that you may know . . . his incomparably great power for us who believe.

EPHESIANS 1:18–19

All-Mighty Warrior, Lion of Judah, Captain of the Armies of Heaven,

Open my eyes to the invisible realm.

Tear away the veil of deception that the enemy has hung over my mind and my heart.

Show me that for every aspect of Your truth,

Satan has a twisted counterfeit.

Give me discernment to detect . . .

His lies in contrast with Your truth,

His suggestions in contrast to Your commands,

His temptations in contrast to Your promises,

His destruction in contrast to Your salvation,

His pleasures that are fleeting,

His plans that are failing,

His purposes that are futile,

And his position that is fraudulent.

239

Thank You that You have not left me defenseless for the Battle.

I choose to intentionally put You on—to hide myself in You. You are the protective Armor provided.

Therefore, I choose to . . .

. . . Wrap myself in the Truth of Your Word so that my thoughts, decisions, and actions are in line with what You say.

. . . Guard my heart with the awareness that I am right with You and to the best of my ability, right with others.

. . . Stand firm on Your Good News that invites anyone and everyone into a personal, permanent, life-saving, life-changing relationship with You through the Cross, and that without Jesus there is no way to come to You.

. . . Trust You in times of peace and times of war; in times of health and times of sickness; in times of wealth and times of poverty; in times of prosperity and times of adversity; in times of life and in times of death.

. . . Claim the blessed assurance that I am Yours and You are mine. I will not doubt my salvation or my eternal security because You guarantee both through the blood of Your Son and the indwelling Seal of Your Spirit.

. . . Take up Your Word as I read it, study it, love it, apply it, obey it, and share it with others.

. . . Pray fully alert for Your Kingdom to come, Your will to be done, on earth as it is in heaven.[2]

I will face the foe with nothing to protect my back because I am not turning around. I will not retreat. I will not back down. I will stand my ground, and having done all, I will keep standing firm.[3]

Saturate me in You . . .

Flood my heart with Your love,

Fill my being with Your Spirit,

Fix my eyes on my Savior, Lord, and King.

Thou art my protecting arm,

Fortress, refuge, shield, and buckler.

Fight for me and my foes must flee;

Uphold me and I cannot fall;

Strengthen me and I stand unmoved, unmovable;

Equip me and I shall receive no wound;

Stand by me and Satan will depart; Anoint my lips

with a song of salvation

And I shall shout thy victory . . .

Cover me with Your blood.

Give me courage to call Satan out when I hear his

mocking, taunting, threatening, derisive, insinuating accusations.

He is a liar. He is a lion.

But You are Lord.

Give me strength to persevere until I see You in death or at Your return. In the encroaching darkness, fill me with Your Light that directs people to the living Hope that is found in You. In a world swirling and swarming with demons, teach me to use the Sword effectively while wrapping it in unceasing prayer. In a world of deception, cleanse my lips and give me holy boldness to speak Your truth so that I share Your Gospel without compromise. Make me a warrior like You.

O Lord,

*I bless thee that the issue of the battle between
thyself and Satan*

has never been uncertain, and will end in victory.
Calvary broke the dragon's head,
And I contend with a vanquished foe,
*Who with all his subtlety and strength has already
been overcome.*
When I feel the serpent at my heel
May I remember him whose heel was bruised,
But who, when bruised, broke the devil's head.
My soul with inward joy extols the mighty conqueror.
Heal me of wounds received in the great conflict;
If I have gathered defilement,
If my faith has suffered damage,
If my hope is less than bright,
If my love is not fervent,
If some creature-comfort occupies my heart,
If my soul sinks under pressure of the fight.
O thou whose every promise is balm,
every touch life,
Draw near to thy weary warrior,
Refresh me, that I may rise again to wage the strife,
And never tire until my enemy is trodden down.
Give me such fellowship with thee
that I may defy Satan, unbelief, the flesh, the world,
With delight that comes not from a creature,
And which a creature cannot mar.
Give me a draught of the eternal fountain
that lieth in thy immutable, everlasting love and decree.

Then shall my hand never weaken,

> *my feet never stumble,*

> *my sword never rust,*

> *my helmet never shatter,*

> *my breastplate never fall,*

>> *as my strength rests in the power of thy might.*[4]

I pray this in the name of the Rider on the white horse—the One whose name is Faithful and True—who one day will return, followed by the armies of Heaven.[5] I pray in the name of the One who judges with justice and makes war, with eyes of blazing fire.[6] I pray in the name of the Victorious Warrior who one day will vanquish Satan, and remove all sin, evil, wickedness, rebellion, hatred, injustice, and lies from this planet. I pray in the name of JESUS.

Grant us victory this day . . .

For the glory of Your Name.

The end of all things is near.
Therefore be clear minded and self-controlled
so that you can pray.

1 PETER 4:7

If prayer is . . . .

One of the supreme joys of life,

The throbbing heartbeat of our relationship with God,

The nearest we will be to God this side of Heaven,

Our compass that helps keep us on the right path . . .

And it is all of the above . . . *why is it so hard?*

The answer?

Because prayer is a battle. A fight. It's spiritual warfare.

It's been said that the secret prayer chamber is a bloody battle-ground.[1] Oswald Chambers stated, *Prayer is not preparation for the battle, it is the battle.*[2]

At the end of this book, it's worth noting that when we pray the Daniel Prayer, we are entering into the realm of spiritual warfare with the enemy. So don't become discouraged when you lack evidence that your prayers are moving Heaven or changing anyone, much less a nation.

Not all prayers are answered immediately. While there are biblical reasons for unanswered prayer, sometimes the answer is simply delayed.[3] There have been many times, after intense, desperate pleading, that I have not received an answer through a verse, nor am I given affirmation through a messenger. And the waiting can be excruciating.

Six years after Daniel poured out his heart to God in urgent desperation for the nation of Judah,[4] he himself went through an agonizing delay to the answer of his personal prayer. He had been given "a revelation," which is the equivalent of saying he was still reading his Bible. He knew that the revelation was God's Word, it was true, and he had enough insight to know that it involved game-changing world events (10:1–2). But he couldn't seem to comprehend what it meant.

During three weeks of Heaven's silence, Daniel went into a form of deep spiritual depression, unable to eat or even to bathe himself. It was as though his very life depended on a deeper understanding of God's Word. And then after a delay of twenty-one days, the silence was broken. An answer was given through God's special messenger. There are three things that the messenger emphasized to Daniel, before he fulfilled Daniel's passionate desire for understanding, that you and I would do well to remember as we pray.

SPIRITUAL WARFARE IS SERIOUS

When the messenger addressed Daniel, he instructed him to "consider carefully the words I am about to speak to you, and stand up" (10:11).

In other words, Daniel needed to "listen-up." And so do you and I. We need to pay attention, not only to God's Word, but to this very serious aspect of prayer. We need to know who our adversary is, what his strategy is, and how we are to protect ourselves defensively while going on the offense against him.

OUR ADVERSARY IS SERIOUS

The Bible gives us a very descriptive picture of our adversary. Peter reveals that our real enemy is the devil himself who is like a roaring lion.[5]

Lions roar when they are hungry, which indicates the devil is highly motivated to hunt you and me down. He is not complacent. Peter says he "prowls," which tells us he is activated and energized as he tries to defeat us. He is not lazy. And he is "looking" because he is totally dedicated to defeating us and destroying our relationships, our witness, our ministries, our families, as well as everything about us. He is not a gentleman. He's more like a no-holds-barred cage fighter. He doesn't lose his focus or get distracted. He goal is to "devour" us, rendering us completely useless to God in our Christian lives and ineffective in our prayers. He's focused. Now that's a serious enemy!

When we pray the Daniel Prayer, the devil will work feverishly to make sure Heaven remains unmoved and nations remain under his grip. But while he is more powerful than we will ever be, we have the authority over him in Jesus' name. Which is one reason, when I pray, I always pray in Jesus' name. He is the One who gives me access into the presence of God and authority over my invisible enemies.[6]

The apostle Paul was well acquainted with spiritual warfare. His entire Christian life was comprised of one battle after another, and one victory after another. So when he gives us clear instructions on how to fight the devil, he is speaking from firsthand experience. As Paul himself was chained between two Roman soldiers, he used the very way they were dressed for battle to describe the invisible armor we are to put on for our spiritual battle, as well as the offensive weapons we are to take up.[7]

OUR ARMOR IS SERIOUS

As we stand firm, unmovable and unshakeable in our position as children of God,

We are to put on . . .

The belt of truth—The first piece of equipment that a Roman soldier put on was his belt, because every other piece connected to it. Without his belt, he couldn't get dressed. Our invisible armor consists first and foremost of the belt of truth which is God's Word. Our entire lives, including our thoughts, actions, belief system, and worldview, are to be reoriented according to God's Word. We are to be saturated in it because it will give us God's perspective in every aspect of our lives. Strap your belt on. First.

The breastplate of righteousness—This was the piece of armor that covered the soldier's heart and his vital organs. The breastplate of our invisible armor is righteousness. Right living. A clean conscience. Which means we need to make sure we are right with God and right with others. We cannot be strong in the fight if we have a deep down nagging sense of guilt. Get right now with God, and as much as possible, with that other person. Your own spiritual health and well-being depends on it.

Your feet fitted with the readiness that comes from the gospel of peace—The soldiers' sandals had cleats on them, so that when in battle they could get a firm footing and were less likely to slip or fall. You and I are to stand firm on the Good News that God so loves the entire world that He sent His one and only Son, that whoever believes in Him will not perish but have eternal life. And His Son, Jesus, is the way, the truth, the life, and no one will come to the Father except through Him.[8] But any and all who will come, may come. That's where real peace is found. We are to be ready at a moment's notice, not only to meet God face-to-face because we have made peace with Him, but to take the Gospel to others so that they, too, are at peace with Him. Stand firm on the Gospel!

And we are to take up . . .

The shield of faith—This was a piece of equipment that was as large as the soldier. And it was only effective if the soldier stayed close behind it. It was almost like a portable wall. Our invisible shield of faith is our total dependence upon God. Our trust in Him. It's key to blunting the enemy's attacks. Again and again, the Bible describes God as our shield, so that if we stay close to Him, we can be confident that any attack that the enemy makes on us will either be prevented from harming us, or will be blunted or softened because it has to come through our Shield first.[9] Just stay close to it.

The helmet of salvation—This piece of armor covered the soldier's head. His thoughts. Reasoning. For us, we are to be assured, without any doubt, that God has forgiven us and that we have received eternal life through faith in Jesus Christ. We will never be victorious warriors if we go around doubting our salvation, unsure that God truly accepts us. Or if we are afraid to die because while we "hope" we are going to Heaven, we are not 100% certain of where we will spend eternity. Put your helmet on!

The sword of the Spirit—While the above pieces of armor are all defensive in nature, the sword is one of two offensive weapons named. While it's obvious that a sword was the soldier's weapon for war, Paul tells us clearly what the sword is when he says it "is the word of God."[10] We are to read, study, apply, and live by God's Word, confident that His Word holds the answers to life's questions and gives us principles to live by that work. It is the written Word of God that supernaturally reveals the Living Word of God, drawing people to the Light, to the Truth . . .to Jesus. We are to take every opportunity to share it with others. Pick it up! Dust it off! Read it every day. Refer to it often. Rely on it. Give it out to others. Wield your sword with the power of God's Spirit, but always wrap it in love.

Then begin to really pray. For a soldier, this would involve his direct communication with his commander. Making sure he knew the battle plan and how he was to proceed. The same is true for you and me. We are not left to guess our way through the battle. We are given direct access to our Commander. To the Captain of the Armies of Heaven. We communicate with Him through prayer. Paul instructs us to "pray on all occasions with all kinds of prayer and requests."[11] Which means you can mix things up as you pray. Your prayers don't have to be according to some prescribed formula. They don't have to be offered in their entirety in one sitting or kneeling position. You can take your music into your place of prayer and begin with your favorite worship songs. Go outside for a walk and thank God for all the blessings you can name. Memorize an alphabetized list of His names and go over each one as you go to sleep. Keep a prayer journal and a prayer list. Use pictures of people, such as missionaries or world leaders, to help you stay focused as you pray for them. Be creative. "With this in mind, be alert and always keep on praying . . ."[12]

Heads up! Are you praying fully armed? Alert to your adversary? Pay serious attention!

SPIRITUAL WARFARE IS SUBTLE

The second aspect of warfare the messenger conveyed to Daniel was more subtle. It was revealed when once again, he addressed Daniel twice in his response, "you who are highly esteemed" (10:11, 19). Did Daniel think because his prayer had not been answered as immediately and specifically as his previous prayer had been, that he had somehow fallen out of favor with God? That Heaven was no longer moved by his prayers?

Is that what you think? When God delays answering your prayer, do you think . . .

That somehow prayer just doesn't work for you?

That God doesn't hear your prayers?

That He's too busy to be bothered with you?

That you are not worth His attention?

That prayer didn't work the last time, so why bother praying this time?

That you're not a prayer warrior anyway?

That the promises of God are not for you so don't expect Him to keep them?

That God's going to punish you by letting you sit in the mess you've made?

Or maybe you think that . . .

You're not special enough,

You're just not that important to God,

You don't have enough faith,

You haven't fasted the right way,

You haven't used the right "formula" in prayer,

You haven't humbled yourself enough,

You haven't claimed just the right combination of His promises,

You haven't prayed long enough . . . or fervently enough . . . or specifically enough . . . or piously enough.

The above list includes just some of the thoughts I have had when answers to my prayers have been delayed. But do you know something? Ninety-nine percent of the time, those thoughts are the hiss of the old serpent, the devil himself, who slithers up and sows suggestions in my ear, trying to undermine my confidence in God. The above list of thoughts are sneaky, subtle lies straight from the father of lies. So I just call him out. I rebuke him with the authority I have been given as a child of God. I claim the blood of Jesus to cover me and shield me from his vicious insinuations and accusations. Then I firmly rebuke him and command him to leave as I keep on praying until I prevail in prayer. Would you do the same?

Has our adversary, the devil, convinced you that God is not answering your prayer because He has not given you what you asked for, the way you asked for it, or when you asked for it? That's subtle.

The devil is a liar. Jesus called him out in a scathing denunciation when He exposed him as a "murderer from the beginning, not holding to the truth, for there is no truth in him. When he lies, he speaks his native language, for he is a liar and the father of lies."[13] What subtle lies has he been telling you? Has he told you that prayer is so hard, it's too hard, so just quit? Listen carefully. Can you hear the hiss of the serpent . . . ?

I wonder what the lie was that the enemy had been suggesting to Daniel? From the messenger's response and tone, it would seem that Daniel had become discouraged and was feeling defeated by the unanswered prayer. Because the messenger immediately reassured Daniel, "Since the first day that you set your mind to gain understanding and to humble yourself before your God, your words were heard, and I have come in response to them" (10:12). That's amazing! Would you claim those words as God's encouragement to you personally? Could it be that God wants to reassure you . . . *From the first day you set your mind to gain understanding through reading The Daniel Prayer, and to humble yourself before your God by praying through the prayers and standing in the gap for your church and your nation and our world, your words were heard, and this book is God's message to tell you . . . God has heard your prayer. Heaven has been moved and nations are being changed, one person at a time.* Praise God! Receive His encouragement, even as you pay attention to one more critical fact about spiritual warfare.

SPIRITUAL WARFARE IS INVISIBLE

I recently heard my dear friend, Priscilla Shirer, describe an experience she had with her youngest son. She related that she took him to a church fall festival where people set up tables with games and fun activities. The most popular game was arranged on the back of a pickup truck. A board was stretched across the back of the truck, with a long cloth covering the board. Holes had been cut through the cloth into the board, and puppets were popping up out of the holes. Steps had been constructed so that a child could climb up and stand level with the floor bed of the truck. The game was played by giving a child a foam mallet that he used to smack the puppets in order to make them stay down in the holes. The game was a homemade version of the Whackamole game I recently saw at our State Fair.

Priscilla shared how frustrated her son had become with the long line leading up to the game. He was tired of waiting, and very exasperated that although the puppets were whacked and whacked, they did not stay down in their holes. So before she was aware of what he was doing, he had released her hand, run up to the truck, and gave a hard jerk to the cloth. It came off. And when it did, three wide-eyed adults were exposed with their puppet-clad hands held high up in the air. While everyone laughed and Priscilla quickly corralled her young son, she was able to detect a spiritual lesson from the incident. The problem with the pop-up puppets was not on the surface. It was not what was readily visible. The real "problem" was underneath in the three adults who were manipulating the puppets. The real problem had been invisible to everyone who was focused on what seemed obvious. Until the cloth was removed and they had been exposed.

The apostle Paul alerted the Ephesian followers of Jesus that spiritual warfare is not against flesh and blood.[14] It's not against something that's visible. The real problem is not obvious. It's "underneath."

With her characteristic humor, Priscilla pointed out that while we may think the real problem is our mother-in-law, our spouse, our teenager, our pastor, our boss, our employee, our sweet tooth, our craving for chocolate—whatever triggers our frustration and causes us to be defeated—the real problem is underneath. It's our enemy. Our adversary. The devil.

When it comes to our nation, we may think the real battle is with a political leader or a form of government or corporate greed or the purveyors of pornography or the abortionists or radical terrorists or the school board or the city council or whatever obvious, visible enemy we can name. While those are unquestionably real problems, the truth is that they are being manipulated by our adversary. Our real battle is not with a visible enemy at all. The real battle—the primary problem—is "underneath" with the invisible enemy. We battle "against the rulers, the authorities, the powers of this dark world, the spiritual forces of evil in the heavenly realms"—the invisible enemy who is manipulating the visible enemies like puppets to do his wicked will.

That's why I am firmly convinced that the primary answer to the mess our world finds itself in today is not politics. Or education. Or jobs. Or the economy. Or legislation. Or democracy. Or capitalism or socialism or communism or Islamism. The primary, bottom-line answer is God—Daniel's God who speaks to us through His Word and listens to us when we pray. Paul warns us that "we do not wage war as the world does. The weapons we fight with are not the weapons of the world. On the contrary, they have divine power to demolish strongholds."[15] As we have already stated, our primary offensive weapons are the Word of God, which is the Sword of the Spirit, and prayer. If you and I want to win the battle against the invisible enemy, we must pick up our Sword as we drop to our knees.

Prayer pulls the "cloth" off and exposes what is taking place underneath in the invisible realm. Which is one reason the enemy fights prayer. He can't be successful if he's exposed. So he wants us focused on the visible. The logical. The obvious. The natural and the temporal. He knows he cannot withstand the Light that is ushered into the darkness by our prayers. So when we drop to our knees, that's when the battle begins in earnest. He will make you feel foolish for thinking you could take God at His Word. Literally. He will try to prevent you from prayer by convincing you that it's not your "gift." You are not a prayer warrior like so and so. Let them pray. That the prayers of one person won't really make any difference anyway. Has the enemy actually convinced you that because God hasn't given you what you prayed for, or when you prayed for it, or how you prayed, that He's not answering? Have you quit? Given up in prayer? Watch out! Can you see what's "underneath"?

The enemy will also try to divert you from your commitment to spend time each day in prayer by a variety of tricks: As soon as you make the commitment, you fall ill. Or your children get sick. Or company shows up. Or you get slammed with the busiest schedule you've ever had. Or your business trip takes you into another time zone that throws off your discipline. Or you get a promotion.[16]

And once you actually keep the commitment and start to pray, that's when the phone rings. Or someone comes to the door. Or the dog throws up on the rug. Or your thoughts begin to scatter all over what you did yesterday and what you have to do today. Or you become so sleepy you can't keep your eyes open. Or you start daydreaming. Or fantasizing. Or planning your vacation. You get the idea, don't you? What tricks has the enemy used to prevent you from praying? Has he played his trump card by convincing you he doesn't even exist?

If Daniel doubted the existence of an enemy who actively sought to hinder his prayers, he didn't after the messenger showed up. The messenger who came to him after the twenty-one-day delay touched on the invisible world in a way that is not only intriguing, but very revealing. He lifted the veil of invisibility that the enemy hides behind —he pulled off the "cloth" when he gave the reason for the delay. He explained, ". . . your words were heard, and I have come in response to them. But the prince of the Persian kingdom resisted me twenty-one days. Then Michael, one of the chief princes, came to help me, because I was detained there with the king of Persia. Now I have come to explain to you what will happen to your people in the future . . ." (10:12–14). Now that sounds like something out of science fiction! Which makes me wonder if even at this moment, the devil is laughing in your ear, and trying to convince you to laugh also. Or at least to skeptically smirk as he hisses that this is fanatical fringe stuff so dismiss it.

While I don't understand all that the messenger said,[17] I do know, and am convinced, that when we pray, we are entering into an invisible, spiritual realm where things are going on that we will never know about until we get to Heaven. That's one primary reason prayer is not easy. Prayer is the front line of the battle.

But be encouraged. When we pray, Heaven is moved! The angelic messenger made that very clear to Daniel when he explained, ". . . your words were heard, and I have come in response to them." Not only did Heaven respond to Daniel's cry, but Heaven rallied to Daniel's cause when the messenger revealed that another mighty messenger, Michael, had come to help in the invisible battle and to insure that Daniel's answer to prayer got through the invisible fog of war.

When you and I pray, Heaven is not only moved, but Heaven will respond and rally to our cause, whether we see visible evidence of it or not. Jesus Himself promised, "I will do whatever you ask in my name, so that the Son may bring glory to the Father. You may ask me for anything in my name, and I will do it."[18]

But Jesus also warned His followers that, "In this world you will have trouble . . . But take heart! I have overcome the world."[19] And because He has overcome, you and I will overcome also. At the end of human history as we know it, when the world melts down and seems totally dominated and ruled by the devil himself, the followers of Jesus will overcome the enemy "by the blood of the Lamb and by the word of their testimony."[20] King David, who was a mighty warrior, revealed the secret of his victories when he exclaimed, "Through God we will do valiantly, for *it is He* who shall tread down our enemies."[21]

The fact that the "battle is the Lord's"[22] seems underscored by the fact that Daniel, battling in prayer, did so with "no strength left," "helpless," "in a deep sleep, with my face to the ground," "trembling," "speechless," "overcome with anguish," "my strength gone and I can hardly breathe."[23] Yet Daniel was victorious!

So . . .

When you fail to consistently keep your commitment to pray, as I have so many times, don't quit.

When you struggle with concentration in prayer, as I still do, don't give up.

When your content seems weak and ineffective, as mine has been in so many ways, keep on keeping on.

Remember . . . this is war!

But be encouraged!

One day, the enemy will be defeated. Finally. Completely. Totally. Permanently. Eternally.

One day the devil will be thrown into the lake of burning sulfur where he will be tormented day and night forever and ever.[24]

One day the golden bowls will be full of incense—the incense of our prayers gathered before the throne of God that trigger the biggest comeback of all time when Jesus returns to claim His right to rule the world.[25]

One day you and I will join with millions upon millions of angels and other followers of Jesus, singing, "Worthy is the Lamb who was slain, to receive power and wealth and wisdom and strength and honor and glory and praise . . . To him who sits on the throne and to the Lamb be praise and honor and glory and power, for ever and ever!"[26]

One day the entire Universe will rock in a victory chant of praise to the Lamb who was slain who has won the victory over all of His enemies.

One day . . . on that day . . . we are going to say every moment we spent in prayer that God used to achieve victory for the glory of His Name was worth it! *Praise God!*

So . . . until that day, keep praying the Daniel Prayer until Heaven is moved and the nations are changed.

For the glory of His Name!

Amen.

THANK YOU, TEAMS!

While writing this book, I was also caring for my husband 24/7. I managed his medications, his meals, his medical appointments, and his social calendar, while also doing my best to minister God's love and encouragement to his spirit. It was a full-time job. Each day, I squeezed into the cracks of time the oversight of AnGeL Ministries and my office staff. While I had ceased to travel, I continued ministry responsibilities through video, audio, and social media. With family time and relationships layered in, I truly was doing much more than I possibly could accomplish in the natural realm. So the thought of adding the writing of a new book to all that I was doing was overwhelming.

As I leaned hard on the Lord, He poured out His blessing, giving me words, thoughts, insights, and stories that enabled me to complete this book in record time. But I would be less than honest if I didn't also acknowledge that God used teams of people to come alongside me in the process, giving me an abundance of practical help. Like the mighty men God brought to David to help him do the work to which he had been called,[1] God has given me teams of people who have helped me complete this project. I would like to offer my public, heartfelt gratitude to:

MY FAMILY

My husband, Danny, who, just before I received back the author proofs, moved to Our Father's House—had he moved earlier, I would not have been able to complete the manuscript. He was keenly interested, and each evening wanted to discuss what I had written that day. I also had the full support of my children and their spouses: Jonathan and Jenny Lotz, Traynor and Morrow Reitmeier, Steven and Rachel-Ruth Wright; and my grandchildren: Bell, Sophia, and Riggin Wright; all of whom were very patient and incredibly encouraging as I secluded myself, disengaging from family activities, in order to write.

THE ANGEL MINISTRIES TEAM

My staff, led by Ross Rhudy, which includes Ginger Kirby, Ava Zettel, Sarah Erwin, Hope Reed, Carol Cooper, Anna Little, Tim Turner, Belinda Sandy, Mary Fuller Sessions, and Jennifer Gillikin as they shouldered the work, freeing me up to spend hours in undistracted writing.

THE PRAYER TEAMS

My personal prayer team, headed up by my daughter Rachel-Ruth Wright, which includes Bonnie Moore, Dody Ragsdale, Bonnie Gaylord, Lynn Roach, Sherry Burrows, Joan Holder, and Debby Morris, who prayed for the Wind of the Spirit to "blow in my sails" when I struggled with writer's block—and the Wind blew. And my Office Prayer Team, led by Beth Murphy, which includes Betsy Batchelor, Holly Yancey, Crystal Yancey, Morrow Reitmeier, and Julia Bryan Canavan, whose intercession secured the smooth running of the office in my "absence."

THE TRANSPORTATION TEAM

Because of my husband's declining health, for over two years nine men consistently came alongside to help me with transportation needs that included 5:30 a.m. pickups for dialysis, and 12:00 p.m. returns. On most dialysis days, they also picked up lunch for Danny so I would be relieved of that midday responsibility. Tommy Drake was the point-man who helped to direct the others: Jim Hendren, Bill Lam, Jeff Burrell, Bo Batchelder, Jim Young, Russ Andrews, Louis Alexander, and Robert Boone.

THE ZONDERVAN TEAM

God undergirded the writing of this book with a group of publishing professionals who were loving, wise, enthusiastic, and very patient: David Morris, Sandy Vander Zicht, Dudley Delffs (who not only did most of the content editing, but also gave the book the working title that became permanent: *The Daniel Prayer*), Londa Alderink, and Bob Hudson.

THE ALIVE AGENCY

Bryan Norman caught the vision for this book very early and helped word the subtitle: *Prayer that Moves Heaven and Changes Nations,* while he and Rick Christian never failed to show me love and prompt attention for anything I needed, whether in the publishing world or on a personal level.

A TEAM OF ONE: HELEN GEORGE

Helen has been by my side since I first stepped into ministry outside of my home. She was my substitute teacher and class administrator when I taught Bible Study Fellowship. Then, when I stepped out to begin AnGeL Ministries, she stepped out with me and has been with me every day since. She has been faithfully and loyally by my side for almost forty years! It's been said that when I start a sentence, she can finish it. For this book, she held off a tsunami of correspondence, fielding phone calls, emails, and other business, so I could have undisturbed blocks of time in which to write. And her eagle-eyed proofing of the pages made her invaluable as the manuscript moved from rough draft to final copy.

While each and every one of the above-named people helped me, they did so because they believe this book will be a blessing to you. So while I thank them, I want to thank you for making their effort worthwhile by reading *The Daniel Prayer*.

POSTSCRIPT

When Solomon finished praying
Fire came down from heaven.

2 CHRONICLES 7:1

INTRODUCTION: IT'S TIME TO PRAY THE DANIEL PRAYER

1. 2 Kings 17:16–23.

2. Daniel 1:7.

3. See note on Daniel 1:3, page 90.

4. Daniel 1:8.

5. Daniel 1:17.

6. 1 Samuel 2:30.

7. While there may have been others praying for God to fulfill His promise, and return the captives to Judah, Daniel's prayer is the only one recorded in Scripture. I believe it is included in the biblical record to teach us not only how to pray for our people and our nation, but to underscore that the prayer of one person can move heaven and change a nation. Ezekiel 22:30.

8. Genesis 6–8; 19:23–29; Joel 1–2; Habakkuk 1–3; Matthew 24:4–8, 29; 2 Peter 3.

9. "Birth Control and Abortion," Abort73.com, www.abort73.com/abortion_facts/birth_control_and_abortion.

10. http://www.ushistory.org/valleyforge/washington/earnestprayer.html; http://www.leaderu.com/orgs/cdf/onug/washington.html

Part One: Preparing for Prayer

CHAPTER 1: COMMITTED TO PRAY

1. 1 Thessalonians 5:17.

2. My husband went to Heaven on August 19, 2015. It's interesting that after forty-nine years of marriage, my commitment to him remains strong—even though he's gone.

3. Daniel 6:10.

4. Exodus 33:7–11.

5. Please visit my website, www.annegrahamlotz.org, and download our ministry app that offers free Bible study materials and devotionals. You can also sign up for our free e-devotional that will come to your inbox every day. It has a Scripture verse and brief application of what it means for life today.

6. Daniel 6:10.

7. Psalm 5:3; 59:16; 88:13; 119:147; 143:8.

8. Mark 1:35.

9. Revelation 3:1–3.

10. Daniel 5:13.

11. Lamentations 3:22–23.

12. Romans 8:18.

13. Daniel 6:10.

14. 2 Chronicles 7:16.

15. Psalm 94:14.

16. Romans 8:28.

17. http://www.gty.org/resources/print/bible-qna/BQ060812.

CHAPTER 2: COMPELLED TO PRAY

1. Romans 7:18.

2. John 15:5.

3. Psalm 46:1–2.

4. Philippians 4:7 NKJV.

5. Philippians 1:6.

6. 2 Timothy 4:6–8.

7. All references to the book of Daniel will be included in the text by chapter and verse.

8. Reprinted as Anne Graham Lotz, *Daily Light Devotional* (Nashville: J. Countryman, a division of Thomas Nelson, 1998). The Foreword of this daily devotional will explain what a meaningful tool this has been in my family as the Truth has been passed down from generation to generation.

9. Haggai 2:4; Ephesians 6:10; Zechariah 8:9; Judges 6:14; 2 Corinthians 4:1; Galatians 6:9 all in the NKJV.

10. Visit my website, www.annegrahamlotz.org, click on *Studies in God's Word*, and then click on *Journey to Jesus*. It's a free resource that will lead you through the steps of how to listen to God's voice. Or use this link to go directly: http://www.annegrahamlotz.org/category/studies-in-gods-word/free-bible-studies/journey-to-jesus/.

11. Genesis 6–8.

12. Genesis 18:16–19:29.

13. Miss Johnson's prayers were instrumental in establishing her international ministry, Bible Study Fellowship, that has brought millions of people into God's Word over the years it has been offered. Mother's prayers were instrumental in my father's ministry as he presented the Gospel face-to-face to over 200 million people in his lifetime, which changed many nations.

14. John 15:5 NKJV.

15. Ezekiel 36:37—God's challenge seems clearer in the KJV: "I will also let the house of Israel enquire of Me to do this for them."

CHAPTER 3: CENTERED IN PRAYER

1. Sometime in January, 2015, Kenji Goto was viciously beheaded by his captors.

2. 2 Kings 4:8–37.

3. Matthew 9:18–25.

4. Matthew 6:6.

5. Luke 5:16.

6. This phrase and this paragraph were adapted from Mrs. Charles E. Cowman, *Streams in the Desert* (Grand Rapids: Zondervan, 1977), 106.

7. Leonard Ravenhill, in Nick Harrison, *Magnificent Prayer* (Grand Rapids: Zondervan, 2001), entry for January 19.

8. Matthew 6:6.

9. Matthew 14:13; Luke 5:16; 6:12; 9:18.

10. Luke 9:2–8. The story of the transfiguration is found in the Gospels of Matthew, Mark, and Luke.

11. This quote is taken from Mark 9:29 NKJV.

12. Matthew 6:16.

13. 1 Samuel 1.

14. 1 Samuel 2:26.

15. The story of Dori can be found in Tom Doyle, *Killing Christians* (Nashville: W Publishing Group, 2015), 43–73.

16. Luke 18:9.

17. The parable is found in Luke 18:9–14.

18. Proverbs 16:5.

19. Isaiah 66:2.

20. Daniel 2:48.

21. Daniel 6:10.

Part Two: Pleading in Prayer

CHAPTER 4: PLEADING WITH CONFIDENCE

1. James 2:17.

2. Hebrews 13:8.

3. Proverbs 9:10.

4. Luke 22:19–20; 1 Corinthians 11:23–26.

5. This alphabetical list is based on Ephesians 1–2.

6. This prayer is based on the following verses: Matthew 24:35; Romans 3:23; 1 John 1:8–10; Acts 3:19; Ephesians 1:7–8; John 6:49–51; 1 Corinthians 11:23–26; John 3:14–18; 1:16; 17:2–3.

7. John 10:28–30.

8. Hebrews 11:6.

9. Lamentations 3:19–23.

10. Job 2:9.

11. Genesis 3:5.

12. Isaiah 43:1–2; Psalm 23:4.

13. 2 Chronicles 33:9–20.

14. While Saul was converted on the Damascus Road in Acts 9, his name isn't referred to as Paul until Acts 13, when he was on Cyprus.

15. The story of the Exodus can be found in the Old Testament book by that name, chapters 1–14.

16. Exodus 14:13.

17. Exodus 14:31.

18. First recorded in Exodus 15:1–18.

CHAPTER 5: PLEADING WITH CONFESSION

1. As the Honorary Chair for the National Day of Prayer 2014, I was asked to write the prayer that was used across the nation.

2. Charles G. Finney, *How to Experience Revival* (New Kensington, Penn.: Whitaker House, 1984).

3. Carol Brooks, "Prayer in Schools," *In Plain Site*, http://www.inplainsite.org/what_happened_when_the_praying.html; and "What Has Happened Since the 1963 Prayer in School Ruling?" *BJU Press*, http://www.christianvssecular.com/higher_standards/prayer-ruling.php.

4. "July 10: This Day in History/1925: Monkey Trial Begins," *History.com*, http://www.history.com/this-day-in-history/monkey-trial-begins.

5. Romans 1:22.

6. Genesis 19:23.

7. Numbers 17:28–34.

8. Romans 1:24.

9. Dr. Al Mohler, *Decision Magazine* (February 2015), 16.

10. Cal Thomas, *Decision Magazine* (February 2015), 15.

11. Romans 1:26–27.

12. Romans 1:28.

13. Romans 1:29–31.

14. Romans 1:32.

15. Joel 2:13–14.

16. James 4:8.

17. Isaiah 5:2, 4.

18. 1 Chronicles 28:9.

19. The most famous lighthouse in North Carolina is located on Hatteras Island and named, appropriately, the Cape Hatteras Lighthouse. Standing 210 feet tall, this black-and-white striped sentinel warns ships of its dangerous locale, an area of the Atlantic called Diamond Shoals, where the Gulf Stream collides with a colder current, creating optimal conditions for stormy seas, giant swells, and shifting sandbars. Over time, the beacon of light from the lighthouse has not grown dim. Instead, at various stages in its history, the power, clarity, number of reflectors, and visibility of the light have been increased. Today, it is clearly visible for twenty miles. And the light has never been allowed to go out. Even during the Civil War it was protected because of its strategic importance to the safety and well-being of the passing ships.

20. 1 Timothy 3:15.

21. Matthew 10:15.

CHAPTER 6: PLEADING WITH CLARITY

1. For a more detailed account, please see Anne Graham Lotz, *Just Give Me Jesus* (Nashville: Nelson, 2000), 44–62.

2. John 2:3.

3. 2 Chronicles 7:15–16.

4. 2 Chronicles 7:15–16.

5. Genesis 18:16, 20–21.

6. Romans 8:27.

7. Genesis 19:15–16, 27–29.

8. John 14:26, 16:12.

9. One of the resources I keep in my place of prayer is a small volume that contains Scripture compilations for both morning and evening, 366 days of the year. The Holy Spirit has used this book more than any other book outside of my completed Bible to speak to me, giving insight and understanding as I pray: *Daily Light with Anne Graham Lotz* (Nashville: Countryman/Nelson, Nashville, 1998).

10. *Charisma Magazine*, March 2015.

11. Revelation 19:11.

12. Revelation 19:14.

13. Revelation 5:11–13.

14. Philippians 2:9–11.

Part Three: Prevailing in Prayer

CHAPTER 7: ANSWERED IMMEDIATELY

1. The story of Honi is based on the writings of Josephus, a first-century scholar and well-respected historian who was born in Jerusalem shortly after the first coming of Jesus Christ. His writings are held in high regard and have been used by the secular world as a very credible source for both Jewish and Christian history.

2. 1 Kings 18.

3. Genesis 32:22–32.

4. 2 Timothy 3:16.

5. 2 Chronicles 7:14.

CHAPTER 8: ANSWERED ULTIMATELY

1. Daniel 5.

2. Daniel was taken into captivity by Nebuchadnezzar in the first deportation in 605 BC. Jerusalem and the temple were destroyed by the Babylonians in 586 BC, approximately twenty years after Daniel's capture.

3. Ephesians 2:19–22; Hebrews 8:5.

4. Hebrews 10:1–4.

5. John 3:16; Hebrews 10:5–10.

6. Revelation 21:1–3; 22:1–5.

7. 1 Timothy 2:3–6.

8. John 14:6.

9. John 17; Hebrews 7:25.

10. John 14:2.

11. Revelation 19:1.

12. Revelation 19:6–7.

13. 1 Timothy 1:15–16.

14. Acts 17:1–6.

15. Isaiah 6:8.

16. Fred Barlow, "William Carey: Missionary-Evangelist," *Wholesome Words* (1976), http://www.wholesomewords.org/missions/bcarey1.html.

17. Stephen Ross, "Charles Thomas (C.T.) Studd," *Wholesome Words* (2015), http://www.wholesomewords.org/missions/biostudd.html.

18. Tom Doyle, *Killing Christians* (Nashville: W Publishing Group, 2015), 1–17.

CHAPTER 9: ANSWERED SPECIFICALLY

1. Judges 6:36–40. The fact that Gideon obeyed, once he was clearly assured he had heard God's Word accurately, gives evidence that he did not lack faith.

2. For those who are curious, my answer was, "Miss Anne. All the men in the office call me that." (And of course, at the time we only had one other man in the office, but that's what he called me so that's what I said.)

3. Isaiah 44:24, 28.

4. Isaiah 45:1–6.

5. Ezra 1:1–3.

6. Ezra 3:7; 5:14.

7. Ezra 4:3; 6:14.

8. Haggai 2:7, 9.

9. Luke 2:22–24.

10. Luke 2:41–50.

Part Four: Patterns for Prayer

PATTERNS FOR PRAYER

1. These prayers are available on my website, www.AnneGrahamLotz.org, under Events or simply go to: http://www.annegrahamlotz.org/events/prayer-initiatives/.

2. In these prayers, the italicized paragraphs, which are also marked with asterisks, are taken from *The Valley of Vision*, a volume of Puritan prayers edited by Arthur Bennett and published by The Banner of Truth Trust (Edinburgh, UK, 2002).

A PRAYER THAT IS CENTERED

1. Hebrews 1:1.

2. Colossians 1:16–17.

3. Hebrews 1:3.

4. Hebrews 1:3.

5. Ephesians 1:20–23.

6. Matthew 11:28–29; John 14:13–14.

7. Hebrews 10:19.

8. Hebrews 10:22.

A PRAYER THAT IS COMPELLED

1. Isaiah 51:16.

2. Genesis 1:3, John 1:1–3.

3. Isaiah 55:9.

4. 1 John 1:5.

5. Deuteronomy 32:47.

6. Psalm 119:89.

7. James 1:17.

8. Ezekiel 36:37.

9. Hebrews 10:7.

10. Philippians 2:6–8.

11. Philippians 2:9–10.

A PRAYER THAT IS CONFIDENT

1. Isaiah 41:10.
2. Exodus 15:11.
3. Psalm 33:6.
4. Genesis 2:7.
5. Colossians 1:13.
6. Psalm 89:1.
7. Deuteronomy 7:9.
8. Genesis 18:25.
9. Isaiah 57:15.
10. Isaiah 57:15.
11. Acts 3:19.
12. Matthew 7:1–5.
13. Matthew 26:64.
14. Luke 23:46.

A PRAYER THAT IS CONTRITE

1. John 8:12.
2. 1 John 1:5.
3. Isaiah 61:10.
4. Ephesians 4:3.

A PRAYER THAT IS CLEAR

1. Psalm 2.
2. Psalm 46.
3. Psalm 40:2.
4. John 14:13–14, 15:16.

A PRAYER FOR THE BATTLE

1. This prayer will be more meaningful if prayed after the epilogue. However, I wanted to include it here with the other patterns for prayer.
2. Ephesians 6:10–18.
3. Ephesians 6:13.

4. "The Servant in Battle," *The Valley of Vision* (Edinburgh, UK: The Banner of Truth Trust, 2002), 328–29.

5. Revelation 19:11–14.

6. Revelation 19:11–12.

EPILOGUE: THE DANIEL PRAYER IS A BATTLE

1. Ole Hallesby, *Magnificent Prayer* (Grand Rapids: Zondervan, 2001), 270.

2. Hallesby, *Magnificent Prayer*, 270.

3. A few of the many biblical reasons for unanswered prayer: unconfessed sin (Isaiah 59:2), arrogance (Job 35:12–13), wrong motives (James 4:3), and so on.

4. He began the Daniel Prayer in the sixty-seventh year of captivity and the first year of the reign of Darius (implying he reigned for at least two years [Dan. 9:1]). The seventieth year, in the first year of the reign of Cyrus, the captives were set free (Ezra 1:1). The prayer he speaks of in Daniel 10 is uttered in the third year of Cyrus, making it approximately six years after Daniel 9.

5. 1 Peter 5:8.

6. John 14:13, 14; 15:16; 16:23; Hebrews 10:19–22.

7. Ephesians 6:10–18.

8. John 3:16, 14:6.

9. Some of my favorite verses from the Psalms describing God as our shield are: Psalm 3:3; 18:2, 30; 33:20; 84:11; 91:4; 115:11.

10. Ephesians 6:17.

11. Ephesians 6:18.

12. Ephesians 6:18.

13. John 8:44.

14. Ephesians 6:12.

15. 2 Corinthians 10:3–4.

16. Interestingly, the devil will use promotion, success, fame, and fortune to keep us from prayer. He will not use demotion, difficulty, disaster, or disease, because those issues will put us on our knees—which is one reason I believe America's prosperity has not necessarily been a blessing from God, because it deceives us into thinking we don't need Him. Not really. So we don't pray.

17. What I do understand is that apparently the nations of the world have invisible demonic rulers assigned to them. Two of them are named: the Prince of Persia (Iran) and the Prince of Greece (10:13, 20). Israel seems to be the exception because as God's chosen people, she has been assigned one of the archangels, Michael, to be her protector (12:1). It becomes fascinating to realize that the

ancient Prince of Persia has once again risen up to come against God's people. That's all I know. Don't get distracted . . .

18. John 14:13–14.

19. John 16:33.

20. Revelation 12:11.

21. Psalm 108:13 NKJV.

22. 1 Samuel 17:47.

23. Daniel 10:8–9, 11, 15, 17.

24. Revelation 20:10.

25. Revelation 5:8.

26. Revelation 5:12–13.

THANK YOU, TEAMS!

1. 1 Chronicles 12.

Wounded by God's People

Discovering How God's Love Heals Our Hearts

Anne Graham Lotz

Tucked into Abraham's biography is the story of Hagar, an Egyptian slave who bore Abraham his son Ishmael. Exiled, abused, and often overlooked, Hagar suffered greatly at the hands of those who considered themselves God's people. Though some of her pain was the result of her own poor choices, there is no doubt that the emotional and spiritual wounds inflicted upon her by those who claimed to follow the one true God scarred her deeply.

Anne Graham Lotz brings the life of Hagar into astonishing relevance. As her story unfolds, you will discover how time and again God acts to help those who have been hurt. But while Anne identifies with the wounded, the unpleasant reality is that she also identifies with the wounders because she has been one too. She knows from experience that wounding is a cycle that needs to be broken. And by God's grace, it can be.

Many have had similar experiences. Maybe you are among those who have been so deeply hurt by the church that you no longer want anything to do with God. Perhaps you are a wounder living in a self-imposed exile, believing yourself unworthy to be restored to a warm, loving relationship with God or His followers. Whatever your hurts may be, *Wounded by God's People* helps you begin a healing journey—one that enables you to reclaim the joy of God's presence and all the blessings God has for you.

God loves the wounded. And the wounders.

Available in stores and online!

Fixing My Eyes on Jesus

Daily Moments in His Word

Anne Graham Lotz

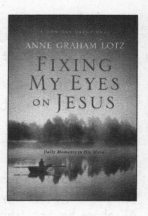

The whole Bible points to Jesus. We need to keep our eyes on Jesus, who both began and finished this race we're in (Hebrews 12:2).

In *Fixing My Eyes on Jesus*, from award-winning author Anne Graham Lotz, you will read a Scripture and inspirational devotion for each day of the year that will encourage, uplift, renew, and challenge you on your spiritual walk with Jesus.

A perfect size for carrying with you on the go, in a beautiful package that also makes this a gorgeous gift for a friend or family member, *Fixing My Eyes on Jesus* is the spiritual nourishment you crave.

Available in stores and online!

Expecting to See Jesus

A Wake-Up Call for God's People

Anne Graham Lotz

Expecting to See Jesus — the expanded edition of *I Saw the Lord* — is the result of Anne Graham Lotz's life lived in the hope of Jesus' return. As you journey with her through the pages of the Bible, you'll come to realize why she lives her life expecting to see Jesus at any minute.

And she wants to make sure you and all other Christians are ready for that moment when your faith becomes sight.

Anne knows from personal experience that it's in the busyness of our days, as we're drifting in comfortable complacency, that we most need a wake-up call — a jolt that pushes us to seek out a revival of our passion for Jesus that began as a blazing fire but somehow has died down to an ineffective glow.

In *Expecting to See Jesus*, Anne points out the biblical signs she sees in the world all around us and shows how you can experience an authentic, deeper, richer relationship with God in a life-changing, fire-blazing revival.

Also Available:

Expecting to See Jesus Curriculum

Available in stores and online!

The Magnificent Obsession

Embracing the God-Filled Life

Anne Graham Lotz

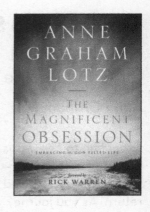

If you or someone close to you is devoted to their church but still struggles to find meaning and passion in their faith; who loves their family, works hard, contributes to their community, but still feels life is somehow incomplete and hollow at the core; who is restless in spirit, with a nagging sense that there must be something more ... there is *The Magnificent Obsession*.

Gifted Bible teacher Anne Graham Lotz, daughter of evangelist Billy Graham, has known these struggles herself. As she studied Scripture, looking for a way out of the emptiness, she found her answer in the amazing story of Abraham, a very ordinary man who became extraordinary for one pivotal reason: he pursued God in a life of obedient faith, not knowing where that decision would take him.

Anne followed Abraham's lead and began a lifelong pursuit of knowing God as He truly is, in an intensely personal relationship. Through personal anecdotes, unforgettable stories, and God-inspired insights, she invites you to draw closer to God, who is as committed to you as He was to Abraham, and longs to call you "friend."

Heaven: God's Promise for Me

Anne Graham Lotz

The light is always on
Because Jesus is waiting for you.
The very best part of Heaven
Is that He's going to be there too.

Heaven is a real place. It's where Jesus lives and waits for those He loves to come to Him. It's a place of joy and love and hope — a place where all of God's children, young and old, will stay and be happy forever.

Engaging questions and Scripture references in the back of this book will help parents reinforce the message that Heaven is a place of love that we can all look forward to seeing one day. There's even a special keepsake invitation for children to RSVP to Jesus!

ANGEL MINISTRIES

Anne Graham Lotz calls people to establish a personal relationship with God through Jesus Christ, then helps them develop and maintain a vibrant faith through His Word.

By visiting www.annegrahamlotz.com, you'll find free devotionals, video resources, and more from Anne's extensive library. Also available are studies in God's Word and access to free Bible study curricula for group and individual studies.